SOCIETY, SCHOOLS & PROGRESS IN CANADA

BY

JOSEPH KATZ, B.A., B.Ed., M.Ed., Ph.D.

*Professor of Comparative Education, University
of British Columbia, Vancouver*

PERGAMON PRESS

OXFORD · LONDON · EDINBURGH · NEW YORK
TORONTO · SYDNEY · PARIS · BRAUNSCHWEIG

PERGAMON PRESS LTD.,
Headington Hill Hall, Oxford
4 & 5 Fitzroy Square, London W.1
PERGAMON PRESS (SCOTLAND) LTD.,
2 & 3 Teviot Place, Edinburgh 1
PERGAMON PRESS INC.,
Maxwell House, Fairview Park, Elmsford, New York 10523
PERGAMON OF CANADA LTD.,
207 Queen's Quay West, Toronto 1
PERGAMON PRESS (AUST.) PTY. LTD.,
19a Boundary Street, Rushcutters Bay, N.S.W. 2011, Australia
PERGAMON PRESS S.A.R.L.,
24 rue des Écoles, Paris 5ᵉ
VIEWEG & SOHN GmbH,
Burgplatz 1, Braunschweig

Printed in Great Britain by A. Wheaton & Co., Exeter

08 006373 X (flexicover)
08 006374 8 (hard cover)

Contents

Geography. Resources. Allegiance. Distance. Culture.
Minorities. Distribution. Identity. Council. Dictionary.
Commonwealth. International.

Explorers. Exploration. The Wars. Westward Movement.
Economy. Resources. Rural Migration. Urbanization.
Industrialization. Transportation. Communication. Inter-
national.

Regions. Provincialism. French Canada. British Canada.
Native Canadians. Stratification. Suburban Communities.
European Influences. Pacific Outlook. Welfare and Medicine.

Enterprise. Departments. Provincial. Larger Units. Trustees.
Teachers. Parent–Teachers. Federal Government Muni-
cipalities. Denominational Schools. Military Schools.

General History. Administration. Curriculum. Programmes.
The Gifted. Creative Classes. Poverty Programmes. Discipline. Playgrounds.

Types of School. Curricula. Holding Power. Revision.
Technical. Technological. Co-operating Organizations.
Government Schedules. Examinations. Administration.
Guidance and Counselling. Inequalities. School Councils.

Comparative Studies

An Introduction to the Series "Society, Schools and Progress"

By EDMUND KING

THIS volume is one of a mutually supporting series of books on SOCIETY, SCHOOLS AND PROGRESS in a number of important countries or regions. The series is intended to serve students of sociology, government and politics, as well as education. Investment in education, or satisfaction of the consumer demand for it, is now the biggest single item of non-military expenditure in many countries and an increasing proportion in all the rest. The systematic use of education to achieve security, prosperity and social well-being makes it imperative to have up-to-date surveys realistically related to all these objectives; for it is impossible to study one effectively without reference to the others or to assess the objectives without reference to education as the chosen instrument.

Comparative studies of all kinds are in vogue. We find university departments of comparative government, law, religion, anthropology, literature and the like. Some comparison is taken for granted in a contracting world of closer relationships. But not all comparative studies are forward-looking or constructive. Comparisons based solely or mainly on backward-looking interests can have their own kind of respectability without necessarily drawing lessons for the present. However, some contemporary comparisons show utility as well as interest or respectability, particularly when observers are enabled to analyse social organization, formative customs, value systems and so forth.

More important still are area studies based upon a comprehensive survey of a whole culture, showing the interpenetration of its technology, government, social relationships, religion and arts; for here we see our neighbours making man—and making him in an idiom which challenges our own assumptions and practices. This concerted and conscious making of posterity by a multiplicity of interlocking influences is perhaps mankind's most astonishing feature—at least on a par with rationality and speech, and inseparable from them. As the last third of the twentieth century begins, however, we are witnessing the struggle of competing educational prescriptions for the whole future of mankind.

THE MAKING OF THE FUTURE

The most important studies of all in the world today are those undertaken with a view to modifying deliberately the formative conditions in which our children and their descendants will live—that is to say, their education. In the pre-industrial past there was plenty of time for the slow evolution of civilization and technology. Even in this century people used to think of societies and education as growing empirically and evolving. Today's world cannot wait upon the spontaneity that sufficed yesterday. It is often said that the Industrial Revolution is entering on its second and more important phase—the systematic application to *social* relationships of mechanized and urban-style abundance, with a corresponding transformation of all learning opportunities.

Certainly that is the dream of the hitherto underprivileged majority of mankind. All countries are involved in this social stocktaking and reckoning for the future, no matter whether they are called socialistic or capitalistic. In any case, the pace of change is so fast everywhere that some co-ordination or phasing of development is accepted as a critical responsibility of statecraft in all countries.

THE TRANSFORMATION OF EDUCATION

In relation to education, this sequence of events has already been attended by remarkable changes. Education used to be undertaken largely at home, by society at large, by working relationships or by voluntary organizations. Now it is a publicly regulated, publicly financed activity for the most part. It is provided as a necessary service by an expanding range of public employees. Of course unofficial people and social groups continue to take a keen interest, especially in their own children; but increasingly it is the State which co-ordinates and directs the process for all children. In some countries the State claims a monopoly of education; in most others that claim is hotly resisted, though inevitably the State is conceded a growing share in the partnership.

In any case, the State or its professional subsidiaries will assume a mounting responsibility for the allocation of funds, for increasingly expensive instruments and premises, for ensuring fair distribution of opportunity, for preventing the waste of talent, for safeguarding economic and social well-being and for setting the national priorities into proper order. Therefore, no matter what education has been in the past, the logic of the Industrial Revolution has turned it into publicly regulated and publicly provided activities, directed towards the deliberate construction of a more satisfactory future.

That commitment is now implicitly indivisible within any one country. It is also accepted that internationally, too, everyone's education is likely to be to the advantage of everyone else in the long run. For this reason alone, international comparisons and assessments are of the utmost importance.

Whole countries are finding that their external context is changing in unprecedented ways. The emancipation of formerly subject peoples is a conspicuous example. Another instance is seen in the large regional developments whereby food production, commerce and mutual protection are ensured in "developing countries"—usually with some notable reliance on educational improvements. Even quite powerful and well-established countries (like several in Western Europe) co-operate increasingly with their neighbours for commercial and political reasons; and all these changes necessitate some adjustment of school orientation and programmes, if only for the interchange of personnel. Apart from such specific instances, it is increasingly obvious that no education anywhere is worth the name unless it is viable in world terms.

Great though these adjustments are between sovereign nations, the changes that transcend all national boundaries and apply to all school systems alike are even more radically influential. In all countries, the area of education monopolized by the schools and other formally instructive institutions is diminishing in relation to educative forces outside. For example, the first public television programmes in the world began in 1936; yet within twenty-five years television and radio absorbed almost as much of children's time and interest (taking the year all round) as the formal school hours in a number of countries. The appeal of such external influences may be greater than the schools'. The universal teacher problem accentuates the change.

In any case, all instruction offered in school is largely conditional for its success on subsequent reinforcement. This it does not always get in a world of expanding opportunities and experiences for young people, which challenge schools' previous prerogatives and sometimes their precepts. A whole new range of "service occupations" provides alternative perspectives. Furthermore, technological and social change necessitate much professional retraining and personal reorientation in all advanced countries. There is far less idea of a once-for-all preparation for life. Learning the unknown is taking the place of teaching the certainties.

In all countries we share this uncertainty. Deeply rooted though we all are in our own ways of life, our scrutiny of the future becomes increasingly a comparison of our hypotheses and experiments. No really adequate answers to any educational or social problem can be determined within one country's confines any longer. Comparative Education is above all the discipline which systematizes our observations and conclusions in relation to the shaping of the future.

COMPARATIVE EDUCATION IN GENERAL

Comparative studies of education are necessarily based upon existing practices, institutions and background influences which have shaped the present variety of educational idioms throughout the world. It is essential to acquaint ourselves with the most important systems, not as alien phenomena but as variations upon the preoccupations of every family and every school in our own country. To be both civilized and scientific we must try to "feel inside" the common human concerns of our neighbours. By this transference of sympathy we achieve some sort of detachment which will enable us to appreciate our own involvement in circumstances—quite as much as theirs.

What adds up to education in our own country is as confused a tangle as any to be found in those countries where we more easily assume the role of critical advisers. Much of it is habituation, and much is emotionally bound rather than rational. Advice and rational planning that do not take account of these actual influences on education at any one place and time are unscientific as well as failing in humanity. From a practical point of view, too, they will fail, because they lack a sense of the local and topical dynamic. We must know the living present. It is this that gives momentum to the future and conditions it. Thus, even at this first or informative stage of Comparative Education, we are made analytically aware (not only descriptively) of today's climax of forces. We inevitably envisage some possibilities for the future— if only with reference to our own reactions and purposes.

Therefore, though Comparative Education must go on to study particular problems (such as control or university expansion), it must begin with area studies or dynamic analyses of concurrent influences such as this series provides. Without awareness of what "education" seems now to be to its participants, no student or planner can effectively share in the shaping of the future. He may have falsely identified his "problems". He will probably misjudge their topical significance. On the basis of unrealistic generalizations he will certainly fail to communicate acceptable advice. The climax of local culture which amounts to education in any one place is emotionally more sensitive even than language issues or religion, because it includes within itself these very influences and many others.

THE PURPOSE OF THIS SERIES

SOCIETY, SCHOOLS AND PROGRESS are here surveyed in the world's most significant countries—significant not simply for reasons of technological or political strength, but because of the widely relevant *decisions* in education now being taken. Since the end of the Second World War a ferment of reform has been going on. No reform takes place in the sterile conditions of a laboratory. In the social field not even research can be isolated and sterilized. Experiment in education involves all the untidiness and unpredictability of human responses, which are the source of all creative ingenuity. Every planner or theorist, every student of "problems" that seem abstract and general enough, needs an opportunity of studying again and again the forensic application of his theories.*

Nevertheless, so that some general study may be made of frequently recurring tendencies and problems, the books in the SOCIETY, SCHOOLS AND PROGRESS series are arranged in a fairly uniform pattern. They all begin with the historical and institutional background. They then go on to describe administration, the school system, family influences and background social forces in much the same order of progression. Thus it is easy to make cross-references from one volume to another. Cross-cultural analysis of particular problems or interests is facilitated, but

* Major problems of decision-taking and implementation are examined fully in E. J. King, *Comparative Studies and Educational Decision*, Bobbs-Merrill and Methuen, 1968.

always in relation to the living context which so often reveals unexpected pitfalls or opportunities.

After this second or "problem" level of cross-cultural analysis in detail, the serious student can go on to a third stage. He can assess as a dynamic whole the collective preparation for the future of each of the countries featured. This third level of assessing orientation, or of planning, is not always marked by logic alone within any one of the countries concerned; but an international survey of discernible trends can be of great practical importance. The evolving form of the future can at least be surmised and continuing research can guide it.

Public investment in education (and consumer demand still more) has often been a precarious venture from the half-known into the unsuspected. Yet buildings, teachers and the children's lives may be committed for generations. For this third level of comparative analysis it is therefore necessary to work closely with specialists in other disciplines, such as economists and sociologists. But the specialist in Comparative Education gives insight and information to them, just as he receives from them. Making the future is no project for any one man, any one discipline, any one interpretation.

This brings us to a last general point. It is more important than ever to have soundly based comparative studies of education, because the relevance of even the best of systems has limits imposed by time. Reorientation and retraining successively throughout life will be the experience of most people in advanced countries for generations to come. That trend is already evident at the most educated levels in the United States, Sweden, Britain and some other countries. All human roles are being transformed, too, not just subjects and occupations. Therefore it is useless to rely on what has been done, or is being done, in schools. We must try instead to think of what will be required, and to observe experiments now being undertaken on the very frontiers of education, where new matrices, new media, new elements and methods of learning are being revealed.

The less settled educational patterns of "developing countries" (where most of mankind live) make it easier for them to be radical. They can by-pass the institutions, methods, and curricula of older-established school systems in their eager pursuit of unprecedented but valid objectives. This is all immediately important to us, because the whole world's educative relationships are being transformed, our own along with all the others. For that reason, one or more of the books in each batch of volumes published in the SOCIETY, SCHOOLS AND PROGRESS series will deal with a developing country, whose experience is particularly relevant in assessing education's contribution to the future.

THE PARTICULAR CASE OF CANADA

Canada lends itself admirably to comparative study, for several reasons. There are, of course, ten distinct provincial systems of education. Within each province are exemplified many of the problems of education to be seen elsewhere: regional and cultural differences; the contrast between city and country, between rich and less well-developed areas; the supply and distribution of teachers and other educational opportunity; the tension between local control and central organization. Moreover, in a country on Canada's scale, these problems are sometimes magnified.

Between the provinces themselves there are distinct differences: of terrain, population density, ethnic and cultural composition, numbers of immigrants, proximity to major industrial and communication centres of the United States, and so on. These contemporary geographical or human differences are accentuated by historical differences. For example, Newfoundland shows the strongest heritage of decentralization derived from the mother country, together with firm links between the school systems and denominational bodies in a multiplicity that makes the "dual system" of some other countries look like no problem at all.

The most notable differences, of course, are to be found between French-speaking Quebec and the other Canadian provinces; but right across Canada a similar problem of cultural and religious idioms recurs, without however being institutionalized to the same degree as in the Province of Quebec itself. To a lesser (but still significant) degree, heavy concentrations of "new Canadians" in Ontario and some other provinces introduce minority problems and questions of assimilation, particularly where the "Anglo-Saxon" element is a diminished proportion. All these cultural, religious, and occupational divergences raise the now crucial question of the "Canadian identity".

This question is all the more cogent because it represents both a historical climax of self-determination and a regional uncertainty related to the United States and its way of life. As the settlement of Canada proceeded westwards, the factors of scale and remoteness and increasingly modern communications lent plausibility to ideas of central administration (within the provincial boundaries) which would have been challenged in the Atlantic provinces, and still more in the home countries of the immigrants. So, despite much local autonomy, provincial standards of schooling and official syllabuses are more acceptable in British Columbia than further east, and secularism in the public schools seems more natural.

All-Canadian needs, from railroads and transcontinental highways to the requirements of higher education and research, challenge the resources of local and provincial governments. In education particularly they may bear upon the relationships of provinces to the Dominion government, excluded as it is from educational interference. Yet provincial boundaries in such a sparsely settled country—itself in places only notionally separated from the United States—make many arguments of self-sufficiency drawn from European countries look outmoded, if not irrelevant.

For Britons and most other non-Canadians, one of the most interesting cultural questions is how far the British heritage and other European traditions have been masked or modified by "Americanization"; and, if this phenomenon has occurred, how far it is attributable mainly to urbanization and mechanization, as contrasted with the directly national idiom of United States schools, colleges, books, and broadcasts. As far as the latter alternative is concerned, most Canadians point proudly to their cultural and educational identity—to the standards of their academic institutions, to the Canadian Broadcasting Corporation, and to several of their journals.

In short, as Professor Katz so ably shows, there is a wealth of material for analytical comparison within Canada itself, as well as beyond the borders with the United States, and with the European traditions which Canadians themselves have developed to a new enterprise.

Author's Preface

Society, Schools and Progress in Canada is designed to provide the reader with an insight into the way in which a wide variety of peoples from around the world have come to live and work together and in the process build a new society. These peoples came to seek opportunities for themselves and their children and for the most part recognized that the key to opportunity lay through education.

Those who came first, the traders and the explorers, and those who accompanied them, the missionaries, came often out of a sense of adventure, a sense of mission, and a sense of romance. Those who followed over the years came to find new social, economic and political horizons and these they found in westward sweeps from the Atlantic to the Pacific and northward from the Great Lakes to the Arctic.

Though American, European and Asiatic peoples have exerted important influences on Canada, and continue to do so, Canada's social and educational history has been determined in the main by the horizons of her French and British heritage. The bilingual and bicultural concerns of Canadians and Canadiens reflect these heritages and promise the pattern of Canada's emerging cultural ethos.

Over the years the schools, colleges and universities of Canada have helped establish a common basis for community and citizenship enabling peoples from many different cultures to find a common purpose and a common destiny. Modern developments in transportation and communication have helped overcome the divisive influences of distance. Nevertheless, this challenge to the viability of confederation remains and may only be overcome by meeting this challenge with imagination and ingenuity. The youth of Canada are in the process of discovering their identity in the heritage of these new horizons.

From the very beginning Canadians have been sensitive to their cultural debts abroad, a sensitivity which has prepared them to appreciate the impact of international perspectives in all spheres of life. In education, as elsewhere, these international dimensions have been at work influencing changes in curricula, in programmes, and in philosophy.

The process of urbanization and industrialization begun in World War I and continued in World War II has hastened the reforms attending the social, economic and political institutions throughout the country. The change from a rural–agricultural to a predominantly urban–industrial economy is reflected in all of Canada's communities and has brought about changes in many a manner and mode of life. These changes, too, have brought with them the problems of people in transition from one mode of life to another. People young and old, native and migrant, skilled and unskilled feeling the impact of innovation have sought and found security in education.

The reader is invited to take this brief journey through Canada in the knowledge that each chapter is but an arch opening up on beckoning vistas.

I want to express my appreciation for assistance to my wife, Mary, always the cheerful critic; to Chris Mewis who kept a watchful eye throughout the preparation of the manuscript; and to Mrs. Stella Wright who saw the volume through its editorial trials. For any errors I alone am responsible.

JOSEPH KATZ

Vancouver

CHAPTER 1

Canada and Canadians

GEOGRAPHY

The northern half of the North American continent is identified on the maps of the world as Canada, a country stretching from the Atlantic in the east to the Pacific Ocean in the west, and from the 49th parallel in the south to the Arctic Ocean in the north. This vast territory, the largest country in the western hemisphere and the second largest in the world next to the Union of the Soviet Socialist Republics, is possessed of long and turbulent rivers, extensive and numerous lakes, immense ranges of mountains, and natural resources in the form of forests, farms, furs and mines. Nature has made it possible for Canadians to have the second highest standard of living in the world, as it has also helped determine a more or less materialistic outlook upon life.

RESOURCES

However impressive nature's endowments may be in giving Canada and Canadians a way of life that is at once distinct and unique, these endowments constitute the background only to a mosaic of peoples whose dominant ethos has been shaped by the English and French cultures over a period of four centuries. The customs and habits of the native Indians and Eskimos have helped form a part of what is the Canadian way of life. But far more important have been the contributions made by European and Asiatic peoples who came and who continue to come to constitute between 15 and 20 per cent of the population. This conglomeration of peoples has not as yet had time in which to produce generations sufficiently unique to be marked by cultural characteristics which separate them on sight from citizens of the United States, or Great Britain, or from France. Canadians when travelling abroad still have to wear a maple leaf brooch to identify their country of origin.

ALLEGIANCE

Although this constellation of peoples has, because of geography and history, become identified as Canadians, there is nonetheless the view, widely held in some quarters, that all too many Canadians are intellectually and emotionally attached to the British Isles, as there are those who are attached by custom and tradition to their native lands in Europe or in Asia. Whereas those of French origin may claim a history of four centuries in Canada, no other peoples outside of Indians and Eskimos may do so. The result of this historical and cultural imbalance in the Canadian polity has given rise to clusters of social, economic, political and religious differences which have at times made the Canadian political confederation a very tenuous affair.

Canada's ten provinces, Newfoundland, Nova Scotia, Prince Edward Island, New Brunswick, Quebec, Ontario, Manitoba, Saskatchewan, Alberta and British Columbia, fall into five major and three minor natural regions. The major regions are the Appalachian (Atlantic Provinces and South-eastern Quebec), the St. Lawrence (parts of Quebec and Ontario), the Canadian Shield (parts of Ontario, Manitoba, Saskatchewan, and Northwest Territories), the Interior Plains (Manitoba, Saskatchewan and Alberta), and the Cordilleran region (British Columbia). The minor regions are the Hudson Bay Lowlands (northern parts of Ontario and Manitoba), the Innuikin region and the Arctic Lowlands and Plateaux (Yukon and Northwest Territories and parts of Quebec). The ranges of climates and resources across these provinces and territories play a significant role in determining the socio-economic patterns of these areas.

DISTANCE

More important than resources or climate is the question of distance in Canada and the part this phenomenon has played and does play in the life of the nation. Newfoundland and Vancouver Island are separated by approximately 4000 miles, a distance which tends to emphasize the historic and cultural differences which shaped each of these islands. Quebec and Alberta are two provinces separated by approximately 3500 miles, a distance sufficient to make it possible for Quebec culture, convention and conception to remain worlds apart from these same domains in Alberta. Whereas French culture and French language guide Quebec, Alberta is guided by a blend of Canadian and American viewpoints. Again both Quebec and Alberta differ significantly from British Columbia, where a predominantly British ethos obtains, and Bruce County in Ontario where Scottish traditions continue to sway local perspectives. The advent of more sophisticated transportation and communication media will go far toward modifying the divisive and isolationist impact of distance and make it possible for proximity to work its cohesive wonders.

CULTURE

The appointment of a Bilingual and Bicultural Commission to look into the relationships which obtain in Canada between and among the various ethnic groups followed upon a belated recognition that French Canada and English Canada were moving apart at an unprecedented pace. What had for long been assumed to be an equal partnership in the Canadian confederation came to be seen by French Canadians particularly as a partnership favouring the English-speaking majorities. Lord Durham's discovery in 1837 in Canada that there were "two nations warring in the bosom of a single nation" was still a fact in 1965, and though the rebellion of 1837 had given way to protests and debates, the dissension was evident politically, economically, socially and culturally. Canadians and Canadiens were aware that some kind of cultural consensus had to be arrived at in order that Canada might remain a viable entity.

MINORITIES

Although French and English views predominate in the conflict of cultures in Canada, there are minority groups large enough to claim recognition of their particular culture such as the Ukrainian, the Polish, the German, the Italian, and the Jewish. These peoples, and many others besides, though recognizing the prior and constitutional claims of the French to a larger slice of the Canadian cake, nevertheless do not want to lose their identity in an amorphous mass. French, English and other components of the Canadian mosaic are all influenced by the American way of life and outlook which reaches Canadians by way of all communication media: newspapers and magazines, radio and TV, and by books and periodicals of all kinds. Despite all of these forces, however, over the years the social, economic, and political forces in Canada have combined to produce generations sufficiently unique to warrant the assertions that a distinct Canadian type now exists and is clearly distinguishable from American and English types. Nevertheless, it is still true that Canada remains a collection of cultures as well as a federation of provinces.

An example of the cultural composition to be found in a school system is seen in the table opposite based on an ethnic survey conducted in Toronto metropolitan schools.

Despite the fact that Toronto has attracted a greater proportion of migrants than have other parts of Canada and the schools reflect this number, other centres in Canada have more or less similar patterns of ethnic distributions in their school populations. In consequence of this pattern of pupils the schools have to be sensitive to the various values these different cultures emphasize and try to accommodate these in all school programmes. In sharp contrast to what one may find in a unicultural society such as Scotland or Japan where the values propounded by the school are those held by the society, the values set forth by a Canadian school may conceivably run counter to those of the home or of even groups of homes. Nonetheless the schools in Canada are managing to establish an ethos capable of illustrating the social, economic, political and spiritual values deemed worthy of emulation in Canadian communities.

Ethnic Survey—English and Citizenship Classes 1965–1966*

Toronto: September–March

Ethnic group	Total
Italian	1642
Greek	1182
Portuguese	550
German	510
Polish	458
Yugoslavian	408
Spanish and South American	142
Hungarian	141
Chinese	136
French	134
Finnish	121
Ukrainian	84
Scandinavian	51
Japanese	42
Czechoslovakian	40
Dutch	38
Total	5679

* Based on *Annual Report, Board of Education*, Toronto, 1966.

DISTRIBUTION

Canada's approximately twenty million people live for the most part along a narrow band of land between the 49th and 60th parallels of latitude. This southern strip along what has been described as the longest undefended border in the world, dips in Ontario below the 49th parallel of latitude—to a point that is south of the northernmost point of California—into what is the Canadian centre of gravity in the most populous and most industrialized part of the country. Although Ottawa is Canada's political capital, it must be noted that Quebec City is Ottawa's counterpart for Canada's French population by habit. Between them, these two provinces, Quebec and Ontario, have more than half the population of the country, and more than half the representatives in the House of Commons and in the Senate. In consequence these two centres of population, Quebec and Ontario constitute the social, economic, and political hub of Canada, and because of this generate waves of resentment from other parts of Canada, resentments which have in recent years given Canada minority governments because Eastern and Western Canadians have seen fit to send opposition parties and politicians to express their resentment in Parliament in Ottawa.

IDENTITY

According to Professor W. L. Morton, one of Canada's leading historians, four factors have combined to give Canada its special character. These four factors Morton identifies as geography; Canada's traditional dependence upon Great Britain, Europe, and the United States; adherence to the monarchical principle of government; and to a constant desire to achieve independence. All four of these factors came into dramatic play when the Liberal Government in 1965 proposed and managed to have accepted a distinctive Canadian flag, the Red Maple Leaf on a white background. The debates which were engendered by this proposal to displace the Red Ensign and the Union Jack on Canada's flag poles reflected the cultural distance which obtained between one part of Canada and another; identified the source of Canada's traditional dependence by revealing how strong were the emotional ties of those who had fought for "King and Empire"; revealed how deeply British institutions had reached into the body politic; and projected onto the political stage all of those young and old of all social and political complexions who believed

Canada was ready to leave adolescence and assume symbolic manhood. The Canadian identity Morton speaks of is, despite all of the weights of custom and tradition to the contrary, a viable entity.

COUNCIL

One measure of Canada's emergence out of its adolescence is the establishment of the Canada Council in 1956 to promote the development of the arts, humanities and social sciences in Canada. The Council provides scholarships, fellowships and research assistance to those engaged in the arts, humanities and social sciences with a view to promoting the growth and development of native talent in these areas. In addition, the Council has a programme of awards to organizations—orchestras, theatres, ballet groups, art galleries, research councils or institutes and similar bodies—all designed to foster the production and dissemination of these art forms throughout the land. The Council also makes it possible to bring visiting lecturers to various universities in Canada, and to enable personnel at these institutions to visit abroad. The establishment of the Council is witness to the desire on the part of the Canadian people to begin to promote and develop the spiritual side of its way of life.

DICTIONARY

Canada's first dictionary of Canadian English appeared in 1962 to help distinguish Canadian English from British and American English. Although Canadian English is for the most part based on its British origins it has nonetheless acquired words and pronunciations of its own, so much so that a dictionary was thought to be justified. Words like snowshoe, Bluenose, bluff, blubber, are native to the Canadian scene and in consequence introduce an element not found in either Great Britain or the United States. The pronunciation of words like roof, house, and others involving vowel combinations again help distinguish

English usage in Canada from that to be found south of the border and from that to be found in London.

COMMONWEALTH

Ever since Confederation became a fact in 1867, Canada has tried to maintain a kind of political equilibrium between the United States on the one hand and Great Britain on the other. Traditionally Canada has attempted to explain the United States to Britain and Britain to the United States in consequence of which Canada has been looked to as the honest broker in this Atlantic Triangle. A part of this equilibrium, however, has been affected by Canada's staunch support of the Commonwealth which apart from any political benefits has enabled Canada to open market and trade channels which otherwise would have remained closed to her. Despite this material benefit many Canadians look to the Commonwealth not only as a source of political and cultural strength but as a counterweight to the immense weight of these forces emanating from the United States. The Commonwealth has helped Canada retain its identity in the face of American cultural influences, and to that extent has continued to exert a force in Canada out of proportion to the weight of the Commonwealth in international affairs.

INTERNATIONAL

When in 1931 the Statute of Westminster gave co-ordinate status to the Canadian Parliament in line with other Commonwealth Parliaments, Canada came of age nationally and internationally, and in doing so developed an image of independence which has contributed to the shaping of the Canadian identity. Although Canada is still tied by an emotional umbilical cord to its motherland, it has nonetheless developed the ability to walk alone in most national and international spheres. Canada's roles in NATO, in the United Nations, in various peace-keeping missions, in Colombo and in Commonwealth assistance plans of various kinds have been growing extensively as measured by the contributions of goods, services and personnel made available to the increasing variety of international agencies which Canada's Department of External Affairs has been establishing. Canadian youth, in concert with youth everywhere, have caught a vision, not only of an international world, but of a non-national world, one in which the basic tenets of Canadian political life, peace, order and good government may prevail for all peoples.

CHAPTER 2

Growth and Development

EXPLORERS

When Christopher Columbus crossed the Atlantic in 1492 he opened wide America's vistas to European social, economic, political and religious hungers, and led the way for a series of explorers who soon found the northern part of the continent, the part that was later to become Canada, as enticing as it was exciting. From the fifteenth through the eighteenth centuries explorers from England, Spain and France probed and plundered their way through the vastness of the northern land. John Cabot came in 1492; Jacques Cartier on several voyages beginning in 1524. In the seventeenth century Henry Hudson, Radisson and Groseilliers, and La Salle found their way into Canada; and in 1731 La Verendrye reached mid-continent, and in 1789 Alexander Mackenzie crossed the continent to reach the Pacific. In the brief span of three hundred years adventurous Europeans crossed 4500 miles of land and water, a distance which in Europe it had taken their ancestors a thousand years.

EXPLORATION

These explorers and others who followed them discovered a land whose resources of fur, farm, forest and mine laid the basis for the rapid advance of peoples from the Atlantic to the Pacific. The discovery and exploration of Canada's fishing grounds, hunting preserves, and mining claims made it possible to establish settlements across the country which continued to attract peoples from abroad. Trappers and traders and assorted entrepreneurs exchanged furs and fish for Europe's axes, guns, beads, needles, guns and liquor. When in 1670 the Governor and Company of Adventurers of England trading into Hudson's Bay began under a charter granted by Charles II there had already been established an extensive trade with England and the continent. By the time the Hudson's Bay Company joined forces with the Northwest Company in 1821 Canadians had already begun to trade as well with the Americans to the south.

Canada's waterways provided the arterial highways for exploration. The St. Lawrence, the Ottawa, the Winnipeg, the Nelson, the Saskatchewan, the MacKenzie, the Columbia, the Fraser, to mention only a few, led explorers and settlers into regions that were later to become the sites for agricultural, industrial and urban developments. With the signing of the Treaty of Paris in 1763, the establishment of American hegemony on the continent in 1776, and the settlement of the War of 1812–14, the conditions for the development of trade, transportation and commerce became available. By 1885 the Atlantic and Pacific coasts were linked by rail and the St. Lawrence River was linked to many communities on the Great Lakes by an extensive system of canals. The settlement of the Napoleonic Wars in Europe, the famines and the depressions which followed in many of the continental countries coincided with the opening of the West in Canada. Between 1880 and 1920 thousands of immigrants arrived in Canada from the British Isles, the Scandinavian countries, the Baltics, and from mid-Europe. This mosaic of peoples helped man the industries of Quebec and Ontario, open new agricultural areas in the Western Provinces and give the developing cities a new cosmopolitan character.

THE WARS

Although Canada has participated in the major wars of the century, the First and Second World Wars, few serious battles have been fought on Canadian soil. During the War of 1812–14 there was fighting in southern Ontario, as there had been in

Quebec in 1759, but no major holocaust has ever served as a focal endeavour for all of the Canadian peoples. Whereas the Americans had the Civil War, and Britons, Frenchmen and Germans have had national crises of various orders since the days of the Romans, Canadians have had to depend solely upon economic and political issues to spell out their national character. The Wars of 1905, 1918 and 1939 did help to shape Canada's role in international affairs, her industrial capacity, and the use of her natural and human resources, but all of these taken together have failed to produce a sharply defined Canadian ethos. The absence of any external challenge to the Canadian ethos has resulted in the development of internal stresses, one form of which is to be found in the separatist movement begun in Quebec and the establishment by the Federal Government of a Bilingual and Bicultural Commission to study ways and means of containing the dissidents and establishing a sounder basis for the union between French and English in Canada.

WESTWARD MOVEMENT

The completion of the transcontinental railway line in Canada in 1885 led to the adoption of a policy of promoting rapid migration of Central Europeans to the West to open up the agricultural lands which lay waiting for cultivation. The completion of the Canadian Pacific Railway and later of the Grand Trunk Pacific, ultimately to be known as the Canadian National Railway, facilitated this migration and led to the establishment of villages and towns on the hitherto unexplored prairies. By the time of the First World War a major portion of the prairies had been settled in those areas where it was possible to grow grain without too much effort. It was in this period that these lands produced the grains for export which led to the West being named the "bread basket" of the world. The provinces of Manitoba, Saskatchewan and Alberta felt the effects of world demands for their grain, and in consequence attracted more migrants from abroad in the 1920's and 1930's. With the coming of the depression in the latter decade, growth and development practically ground to a halt across Canada, affecting Western Canada in the same way. The province of British Columbia while benefitting from these early movements and developments didn't really come into its own until the Second World War when Canada's role in the Pacific drew the attention of many servicemen and entrepreneurs to the advantages of a wealth of resources in a West coast climate.

ECONOMY

Canada's economic development began with Cabot's discovery and exploitation of the fishing grounds off Newfoundland. This industry has continued on this island and has developed also in the Atlantic Provinces and on the West coast. Freshwater fishing has also assumed sizeable proportions on the Great Lakes and on the lakes of the Western Provinces. The fur industry followed in the seventeenth century and to this day provides for a considerable addition to Canada's earnings, much of this from catches in the Northland to which most animals have retreated before advancing settlements. The fur industry has been modified, too, by the development of fur farms and these have been adding considerably to the fur dollar.

The period following the establishment of British rule in 1763 was characterized by consolidation, settlement and westward movement. The increase in agricultural settlement in the early 1800's and the extension of roads, canals and rails made wheat a central part of the economy by the 1900's. Between 1900 and 1950 there was a rapid expansion in production of minerals and newsprint. The industrial capacity of the nation continued to increase in the form of manufacturing of farm implements, furniture and the like, but in the main Canada continued to rely upon the United States for its manufactured goods. The demands of the Second World War had given Canadian industry a further opportunity for development, but again, despite significant growth behind a protectionist policy, most goods used in Canada were manufactured in the United States, Britain, Europe and Japan. The sixties witnessed an increase in the number of manufacturing enterprises begun in Canada, particularly British Columbia, by Japanese commercial and industrial interests attesting to this country's ingenuity and imagination. One result of Canada's remaining essentially an exporter of primary unprocessed products has been the continued drainage of its skilled manpower to the United States. This drain of skill has been of the order of some five hundred people a month for the past two decades, a loss which Canada seeks to replace by seeking emigrants with skills abroad. Unfortunately, many of these arrive and use Canada as a stepping-stone to the American labour market.

RESOURCES

Canada's economy has yet to take full advantage of all the resources to be found in the country. The production of metal and non-metallic ores, of oil and gas, of wood and fibre products has brought prosperity to many, but it has not brought with it a commensurate development in secondary industries. Canada's water and power resources are sufficiently extensive to ensure plenty for several generations given present levels of usage, but these resources however well developed over the years have not stimulated a comparable development in industry. The growth and development of the agricultural sector of the economy has been marked by a continuing increase in primary production without a comparable development in the secondary area. This pattern of resource development over the years has had its effect upon the development of the educational system. One result was the postponement of the emphasis upon vocational and technical education throughout the country and a much belated attempt to catch up in the sixties by embarking upon a vast technical school building programme, when it first became evident that what industrial development was beginning to take place was being hampered by a lack of skilled people. It very soon became clear to many that while natural resources could be developed with comparatively unskilled people the same was not true when the economy began to move toward secondary industry.

RURAL MIGRATION

Canada's population of some twenty million people has become in the 1960's largely an urban population. Whereas at the turn of the century about 90 per cent of the people lived on farms, by 1931 only about one-third was so resident, and by the 1960's about one-quarter. This shift in population placed strains upon urban centres, but in no way affected the productivity of the farm which had been showing steady increases attributable to more scientific farming and increased use of mechanical methods. The migration of young people from rural to urban Canada altered the character of both types of community resulting in a shift in social and economic patterns. To a degree also political patterns changed upsetting the balance in provincial legislatures to the degree that urban centres are still under-represented and votes in rural centres are worth double or triple those in urban communities. Because the average age of the population in rural communities has been rising as a result of the migration of young people, the conservative character of rural areas has been enhanced to the extent that the political disparity between rural and urban areas has been increasing.

URBANIZATION

In the decade between 1951 and 1961 Canada's major urban centres showed a remarkable increase in population, over thirty cities reaching populations ranging from fifty thousand to two million. Despite this concentration of population, however, the number of people per square mile in Canada still averages only about $5 \cdot 12$ even though the densities of cities range from 5000 in Ottawa to 25,000 in Montreal the largest city in Canada.

The process of urbanization has varied from one part of Canada to another. In Ontario and Quebec urbanization has been speeded by a high rate of industrialization, a pace greater than that to be found elsewhere in Canada. In predominantly agricultural provinces such as Saskatchewan, New Brunswick and Manitoba, urbanization has been somewhat slower, matching the slower rate of industrialization. In this decade too the pattern of migration has shown itself to be one moving in the direction of urban areas reflecting the influence of large European concentrations upon the mobile populations seeking new climes and cultures.

The impact of urbanization upon the organization and administration of education in Canada is to be seen in developments taking place in the form of the emergence of divisions of higher education in Departments of Education; the establishment of junior and community colleges; the increase in the number of vocational and technical schools and colleges; concern with the special educational provisions necessary for children in underprivileged areas; the increase in provision for children of preschool and kindergarten age; and, the attention being given to the retraining of adults whose jobs have been affected by automation and the computer.

INDUSTRIALIZATION

Ontario continues to maintain its position as the leading manufacturing province in Canada, followed by Quebec, the Prairies, British Columbia and the Atlantic Provinces. The process of industrialization has followed closely the development of power resources such as coal, water and oil, the processing of raw materials such as iron ore and forest products, and the identification of markets brought close by transportation or created by immigration.

Although the process of industrialization had already begun to develop in Eastern Canada by the time of Confederation in 1867, manufacturing was slower in coming to the fore in Western Canada which, even to the present, remains essentially a primary producer despite heroic efforts to industrialize. The development of power resources in the prairies, and in British Columbia, and the development of markets in the Pacific are hastening the development of industrial projects in the West.

Industrialization has brought with it greater attention to vocational and technical education. The development of technological institutes has paralleled the development of the industrial complex and though these institutes were in some instances late in developing they nevertheless did help to prepare people for emerging industries. In one instance a technological institute has been opened to provide training facilities for handicapped who can then take their place in the world of work. In other instances industrial and commercial organizations are developing special training and retraining programmes for their own employees.

TRANSPORTATION

Canada's social, economic and political development has depended to a very large degree upon the provision of adequate transportation. With a land mass greater than that of the United States, a distance of forty-five hundred miles from the Atlantic to the Pacific, and a relatively sparse population spread mainly along the southern border adequate transportation has always been critical to any kind of development. Confederation itself came into being in part as the basis for establishing a railway to improve upon the poor communication provided by corduroy roads and a poor system of canals.

Canada's growth followed closely the growth of railway systems, the opening up of new roads, the introduction of the motor car, and ultimately the airplane. In the past century the ability to move the products of the factory from anywhere in the interior of the country to any coast and any market has altered radically the potentiality of the various communities for the development of industry. Today most communities in Canada, if they have the resources, can entertain plans for the development of industry since transportation as such would pose few problems.

COMMUNICATION

Communication in Canada has been and is critically important
to the development of a sense of community. This sense of community, originally contributed to by the voyagers, the roads and
the railways has since been further developed by the advent of the
telegraph, the telephone, and by radio and TV. The existence of
some six million telephones in Canada making quick communication possible between the Atlantic and the Pacific, and between
the Arctic and the American border has made it possible in some
respects to overcome some of the problems posed by distance
alone.

The development of telex systems, radio telephones, closed-
circuit TV systems, teletypewriter systems, and the like fruits of
technological progress have all helped shape an attitude of mind
regarding distance in Canada which has gone a long way to
breaking down resistance to opening up some of the remote areas
of the country. As stated in the *Canada Year Book*, 1965:

> "Great networks of telephone, telegraph and radio services, inextricably
> bound together, provide adequate and efficient service which, in this era
> of electronic advancement, is under continual technological change and
> development. The familiar challenges of the country—its size, its topo-
> graphy, its climate, its small population—which have reared their heads
> in other areas of development, have had to be faced as well in the field of
> communications."*

All of these developments have been reflected to a considerable
degree by matching developments in the emergence of technological institutes in Canada designed to provide the technical
experts required by communications systems in constant need of
people knowledgeable in radio services, electronics, electricity,
microwave installations, television and so forth.

The Canadian Broadcasting Corporation operates 39 radio and
TV stations across the country, while the Canadian Television
Network, a consortium of private stations, operates 267 radio

* *Canada Year Book, 1965*, p. 824.

stations and 158 TV stations. Since 1918 when the first radio broadcast took place in Canada radio and television services have expanded so as to reach approximately 98 per cent of the people. Today even the remotest village in the Arctic has access to radio news, though television reception is not so far widespread.

There are in all some 116 daily newspapers in Canada, and these report an aggregate circulation of just under four and a quarter million copies. About 82 per cent of this circulation reaches the English community; 18 per cent the French. In addition there are 671 weekly newspapers which serve more people in the rural areas than do the dailies and cater to local interests to a very considerable extent. Newspapers are also published in several languages by the foreign-language press including Byelorussian, Chinese, Croat, Czech, Danish, Dutch, Estonian, Finnish, German, Greek, Hungarian, Icelandic, Italian, Japanese, Latvian, Lithuanian, Macedonian, Maltese, Norwegian, Polish, Portuguese, Russian, Serbian, Slovak, Slovenian, Swedish, Ukrainian and Yiddish. In all the foreign language press publishes 102 separate papers.

Despite the entry of a tremendous number of publications from the United States, Canada still does produce a number of magazines of its own. In 1963, for example, there were in Canada 57 periodicals devoted to agricultural and rural matters; 40 to the arts, crafts and the professions; 20 to construction; 99 to education; 13 to finance and insurance; 29 to government services; 48 to home, social and welfare; 14 to labour; 40 to pharmacy and medicine; 37 to religion; 69 to sports and entertainment; 197 to trade and industry; and 42 to travel. This distribution reflects the various categories of interests to be found in the economy, and provides still another index as to the opportunities available to students who graduate from school at any level.

INTERNATIONAL

Canada's international independence began to take shape when in 1922 Canada signed the Halibut Treaty with the United

States and Britain recognized Canada's right to do so. In 1931 with the Statute of Westminster, the Canadian parliament became an independent body and moved toward international recognition as an independent political entity. Canada's role in two World Wars, in the League of Nations, in the United Nations, in Unesco, and in the International Development Bank has been one to draw the attention of the world to Canada's desire to become known as a peace-maker, as well as a middleman.

Canada's multi-cultured mosaic has helped her in shaping international policies which make their appeal to many peoples around the world. The fact that Canada has never had any colonies, and apparently doesn't aspire to any has predisposed many emerging nations to look to Canada for advice and assistance regarding economic, political, educational and technological matters. Canada's readiness to accept responsibility for peace-keeping operations in many parts of the globe; her willingness to compromise in order to maintain the peace and recognize the legitimate claims of others; her desire to accord each peoples a just place in the international scheme of things, these and other like activities on the international scene have brought Canada to the attention of the world of international affairs.

Canada's interest in international education takes the form of six programmes administered by the Department of External Affairs: the Colombo Plan, the West Indies Programme, the Commonwealth Technical Assistance Programme, the Canadian Commonwealth Scholarship and Fellowship Programme, the Special Commonwealth Aid to Africa Programme, and the Canadian Programme of Educational Assistance for the French-speaking States of Africa. Canada's international education efforts are furthered also by the Canadian University Service Overseas, a voluntary agency supported by students and business men since 1961; by the Company of Young Canadians, a government sponsored agency along the lines of the Peace Corps; by bilateral arrangements entered into by universities at home and abroad; and, by programmes sponsored by Canadian National Commission for Unesco, the Canadian Teachers' Federation, and by the Canadian Education Association. Despite these apparently energetic efforts, Canada's involvement in educational activities abroad are relatively minimal considering the country's resources and potential.

CHAPTER 3

Canadian Communities and Societies

REGIONS

The forty-five hundred miles of Canada which separate the Atlantic from the Pacific fall into five main regions. The Atlantic Provinces include Newfoundland and Labrador, Nova Scotia, New Brunswick and Prince Edward Island. This region is settled by people whose ancestors arrived at various times since the sixteenth century from England, France, Ireland, Scotland and Germany, and who have managed to retain their several strong traditions intact. In Cape Breton and Nova Scotia, for example, the Gaelic dialect and highland and lowland customs are still to be found interestingly enough in a climatic and topographical setting reminiscent of the homeland. Prince Edward Island, on the other hand, still retains the flavour of eighteenth-century England and customs and traditions stemming from these days are still extant in the island.

Quebec constitutes a separate and distinct region of its own. Although predominantly French, the English, Jewish, and mid-European elements to be found in the population lend a cosmopolitan character to the area. This region is characterized by a distinctive French way of life including the use of the French language, a seventeenth-century patois which has become current; a unique French oriented culture including literature, theatre, handicrafts, social life, and family conclaves. Until the period of the Second World War, the majority of the Quebec population was rural in character. Since then, the advent of industry, the development of the natural resources of the province, and the recognition that science and technology were essential for tomorrow, Quebec's leaders in all sectors of the economy have

22

helped move Quebec out of the nineteenth into the twentieth century. Nevertheless, there are a sufficient number of pockets in the population who have sought to stem the advancing tide of change.

Ontario constitutes the third major geographic and cultural region in Canada. Originally settled by migrants from England, Ireland and Scotland, the region, the most heavily industrialized in Canada, has attracted many Europeans in waves of migrations preceding and following the Second World War. This region, which stretches for about a thousand miles between Quebec and Manitoba, borders the Great Lakes and Hudson's Bay, possesses vast resources of minerals, has the greatest numbers of metropolitan centres, and the largest concentration of population. Ontario possesses, too, the centre of finance, publishing and commerce, and though several aspects of these are shared with Quebec, most of the major policy decisions governing the industrial and commercial communities emanate from here. With the capital of Canada located in Ottawa, Ontario, and the surrounding constellation of government offices and agencies, it is easy to see that the industrial, commercial and financial sectors of Eastern Canada have a ready access to sources of decision.

The provinces of Manitoba, Saskatchewan and Alberta constitute the fourth major region in Canada, usually referred to as the Prairies. These stretch for approximately a thousand miles between Ontario and the Rocky Mountains on Alberta's western border. Explored early by La Verendrye, settlement did not begin until 1811 but then spread rapidly westward. By 1905 all of these provinces had been incorporated in the Canada established by the B.N.A. Act in 1867. The Prairies, often referred to as the bread basket of the world, have also become famous for producing oil in Alberta, potash in Saskatchewan, and Goldeye in Manitoba. The population of the Prairies has never been heavy, tending to remain at about the three million mark achieved during the Second World War.

The province of British Columbia on the Pacific coast is characterized by mountainous terrain in which valleys provide for rich fruit-growing areas; mining; grain and cattle growing. This province is rich in natural resources particularly forests, and in the water power needed to develop these. The province did not attract many residents until the Second World War, but since then has been growing at a rapid rate. Because this province is on the Pacific coast, its business men have begun to look to the Pacific basin for their large market instead of to Eastern Canada; and, too, for the same reason, British Columbians have always felt a particularly close affinity for their American neighbours on the West coast in Washington, Oregon and California. The approximately one thousand miles of mountains which lie between the coast and the prairies represent a psychological as well as a physical barrier.

The Yukon and the Northwest Territories bordering on the Arctic Ocean and stretching from the Pacific to the Atlantic across the northern borders of Canada's provinces constitute the large northland of Canada which is relatively underdeveloped. Though Indian and Eskimo have wrestled with the forbidding terrain and climate for aeons, it is only within the past two decades that Canadian federal and provincial governments have looked north to developing the resources of the area. The results of the exploratory activities of oil and mining companies have been such as to warrant the development of the region by the country as a whole.

PROVINCIALISM

Although the regional divisions of Canada have helped to modify the worst effects of the provincialisms engendered by the political boundaries established by the British North America Act, there has not been enough modification to enable an observer to ignore them. One result of the establishment of provincial legislatures with powers and responsibilities exclusive of federal jurisdiction has been the narrowing of the vision of the governors and residents of each of the provinces. The past century has witnessed the development of provincial powers at the expense of

the Federal Government with the result that the concept of
Canada has receded before the onslaught of provincial rightists.
In consequence of these political developments social, economic
and educational outlooks have been similarly affected. The
Atlantic Provinces have since Confederation believed that Canada
as a whole ought to compensate their peoples for lack of natural
resources, and for lack of industrial developments. At the same
time the residents of the Maritime Provinces have done little to
sink their own regional differences or done much by way of
adapting their way of life to the significant changes taking place
to the south and east of them. By the same token the peoples and
governments of Quebec and of Ontario have maintained many of
the antipathies developed in the eighteenth and nineteenth centuries. The governments of the Western Provinces have traditionally been political mavericks indicating that this region is not
always in sympathy with federal policies oriented more towards
the needs of Central and Eastern Canada. The provincialism of
the peoples of British Columbia stems from quite another source,
a sense of remoteness from the sources of political and economic
power in Eastern Canada, and a population complex that is more
oriented to Ontario and the Maritimes and England than to
other areas in the country. Taken all together these several and
distinct forces have given Canadians a set of provincial outlooks
which federal policies and programmes have failed to conquer.

FRENCH CANADA

French Canadians constitute a cultural entity in themselves.
Though primarily located in the province of Quebec, there are
sizeable French communities in Ontario, Nova Scotia, New
Brunswick, Manitoba, and to a much smaller extent in the
remaining provinces. All of these French communities recognize
a common language, a common religion, a common value system
to so great a degree that all of the peoples who participate in this
commonalty constitute a separate society. Quebec's political
parties have all had to recognize what has become known as the

French fact in negotiations with the Federal Government. More recently, the Quebec government has been engaged in negotiating closer liaisons with Paris and French peoples throughout the world. The Canada Council in its assessment of the state of cultural activity in Canada paid tribute to the fact that French Canadian expenditures on music, art, literature and handicrafts surpassed by a considerable margin the expenditures on the same fields in the rest of Canada.

The appointment of a Bilingual and Bicultural Commission in 1965 pointed up the degree to which the separatist movement—a movement designed to gain economic and political equality for French-Canadians either in or out of Confederation—had gathered strength not only in the province of Quebec but in other provinces of Canada as well. The dissatisfaction of the French with the crumbs which had fallen to them from the British establishment in Canada was soon matched by equivalent statements of dissatisfaction from other minority groups in the country.

BRITISH CANADA

Although the English, Irish and Scottish people among them constitute only 43 per cent of the total population, the influence exercised by this British stock in government, finance and commerce is greater than the figure itself would suggest. The French with 30 per cent of the population do not exercise the proportionate amount of influence. It was this imbalance which ultimately led to protest movements of various kinds. The next largest group in the population is German followed by the Italians and the Ukrainians. The Canadian mosaic is rounded out with peoples from Austria, Belgium, Denmark, Finland, Greece, Hungary, Iceland, Israel, Lithuania, Norway, Poland, Rumania, Sweden, and Yugoslavia. Between 2 and 3 per cent of the population are oriental, mainly Chinese and Japanese, and between 1 and 2 per cent are native Indians and Eskimos. This mixture in the population has made it relatively easy for the homogeneous cultures, the

British and the French to maintain their relative dominance in the government of the country; the French influence, however, has been until recently, pretty well confined to Quebec. With the strength of the separatist movement gaining ground, however, more French influence is being felt across the country and at all levels in government, business and industry.

NATIVE CANADIANS

Canada's native population is made up of approximately 210,000 Indians and about 10,000 Eskimos. The Eskimo population is distributed across the northland bordering on the Arctic Ocean. The Indian population for the most part is located on reservations where they are considered wards of the government and treated accordingly. These native peoples have been restless under this yoke and have been agitating for a new status. As in other segments of society the young people, Eskimo and Indian alike, are anxious to achieve a status which will enable them to take their place in society along side those of other cultures. Although about 25 per cent of native Indians and Eskimos do not live on reservations the attitudes toward this group are coloured by deprecatory attitudes of many toward the dependent natives. The policies of the Department of Northern Affairs which has jurisdiction over the Eskimo peoples, and the policies of the Department of Indian Affairs have in recent years been changing from one of containment to one of absorption in the Canadian way of life.

STRATIFICATION

The income statistics of the Department of National Revenue for 1962 showed that there were in Canada in that year: 86,585 farmers who were assessed for $389 million; 4836 fishermen assessed for $25 million; 4390 accountants; 14,169 medical doctors; 4653 dentists; 7703 lawyers; 2546 engineers and architects; 4,090,943 employees; 54,441 salesmen; 195,599 business proprietors; 133,052 investors; and 51,220 pensioners. Of the total number of taxpayers in Canada in 1962, only 3,606 paid taxes on incomes of $50,000 or over; 17,112 on incomes over $25,000; and 160,128 on incomes over $10,000. From the foregoing distributions Canadian society may be adjudged predominantly middle class, and what stratification does occur is essentially ethnically and economically based. Canadian socially aspiring foxes and vixens have not really been blooded!

SUBURBAN COMMUNITIES

The rural–urban distribution of population varies from province to province. In two of the provinces, Saskatchewan and Prince Edward Island, the ratio of rural to urban population is of the order of two to one; this ratio also holds in two of the territories, the Yukon and the Northwest Territories. In three of the provinces, Newfoundland, Nova Scotia and New Brunswick, the ratio is one to one. In five of the provinces the urban population is greater than the rural: in Manitoba and Alberta the ratio of rural to urban is one to two; while in Quebec, Ontario and British Columbia the ratio is one to three. As is to be expected, it is in the last five provinces that one finds the largest suburban populations as well. These differences in the distribution of population have stimulated differences in response to federal proposals and political issues. The provinces on the Atlantic coast and on the Prairies have considered themselves the have-nots and argued their cases accordingly. Today, as in the past, the political parties in these provinces do not necessarily see eye-to-eye with their federal counterparts.

EUROPEAN INFLUENCES

The character of Canadian communities has been altered from time to time by the influx of immigrants from Europe and Asia. In 1963 some 25,000 immigrants from England, Scotland, Ireland and Wales; 15,000 from Italy; 7000 from Germany; 5000 from Greece; 4000 from Portugal; 3500 from France; and 12,000 from the United States. Egypt, the Netherlands and Poland each sent about 1500; while less than a thousand each came from Hungary, Spain, Switzerland, Yugoslavia, and Israel. A few other countries were represented to make for a total of 93,151 entrants to Canada. By far the largest proportion of these immigrants came to reside in Quebec and Ontario, with the next largest groups settling in British Columbia, Alberta, Manitoba and Nova Scotia. According to the most recent Canadian census: "of the male workers, 22·2 per cent were classed as professional and managerial; 7·5 per cent were in agricultural occupations; 6·1 per cent in service occupations; 4·8 per cent in manufacturing, mechanical and construction trades, and 11·0 per cent were general labourers."* From the foregoing it is evident that the largest number of immigrants would settle in urban communities and affect the total outlook and complexion of these areas. The addition of considerable numbers of skilled tradesmen, electroplaters, cabinet and furniture makers, brick and stone masons, printers and pressmen, butchers and meat cutters all reflecting the customs, traditions, and expectancies of their individual homelands is bound to give each community a colour and cultural constellation markedly different from what preceded the influx. Needless to say value systems normally taken for granted are challenged if not directly at least by way of example.

PACIFIC OUTLOOK

It has become increasingly clear in the past two decades that the westward movements of peoples is repeating itself in Canada. Despite the fact that the industrial heart of the country in Quebec and Ontario continues to attract the greatest number of immigrants, increasingly large numbers later move to the more temperate climates to be found in Alberta and British Columbia. This westward movement in Canada has been motivated in part by the change in the life styles of Japan, China, India, Malaysia and the Philippines which have brought about an increase in

* *Canada Year Book, 1965,* p. 213.

trade with Canada. Though the bulk of Canada's part of the trade is made up of raw materials, an increasing proportion is being made up of manufactured items. On the other hand the Asian countries, particularly Japan, have been industrializing at a rate great enough to show up significantly on their export lists. More recently they, and especially Japan, have been sending skilled technicians abroad to establish manufacturing plants employing Japanese know-how and techniques. The industrial interests of Japan and British Columbia have been finding common cause in the realm of commerce and finance. It is entirely likely that in the foreseeable future the exploding Pacific basin will trigger a commensurate development on Canada's Pacific coast. It is equally likely that the states of Washington, Oregon and California will respond in the same way.

WELFARE AND MEDICINE

A 50 per cent increase in the Canadian population in a decade has posed many problems for a society that has been changing rapidly in terms of urban–rural ratio, rate of industrialization, technological developments, transportation and communication media, and immigration and emigration patterns. When to these changes there are added those of new conceptions in social work, health and physical development, medical, mental and dental health care, it is evident that the general attitude of society toward the individual has changed significantly. Particular attention has been given to the needs of children by way of Family Allowance cheques which each child between birth and adolescence receives each month to help assure adequate food, health and clothing. Pensions shared by federal and provincial governments are paid to all citizens sixty-five years of age and over. The Federal Government also subsidizes a variety of health schemes, physical and mental health education programmes, and rehabilitation and child care centres. A national health grant programme also provides for the development of hospitals, the maintenance of veteran hospitals, and research programmes of all kinds in the realm of medicine. Over the past three decades allowances have been made available for the unemployed, the physically disabled, the blind, the chronically ill, and for those who require retraining and reeducation of one kind or another. Food and drug controls, hygienic standards, alcohol and venereal disease controls are all provided for by programmes shared by both federal and provincial authorities. To an increasing degree, the results of scientific and medical studies, of social, psychological and psychiatric studies are finding their way as guides to political action in Canada. At present a significant portion of the tax dollar is devoted to health and welfare programmes of all kinds with effects which are evident in the youth of the nation particularly.

CHAPTER 4

The Educational Enterprise

ENTERPRISE

The educational enterprise in Canada involves three and a half million children in elementary schools; over one million in secondary schools; one hundred and eighty thousand students in colleges and universities; one hundred and sixty thousand teachers in elementary and secondary schools; thirteen thousand professors of various ranks in higher educational institutions; and some fifty thousand trustees. In all something like a quarter of the population of Canada is engaged full or part-time in the business of education, a proportion which is by itself indicative of the regard accorded education in the society.

DEPARTMENTS

Primary responsibility for the organization and administration of the educational enterprise falls upon the provincial legislatures who according to Section 93 of the British North America Act of 1867 have sole and exclusive jurisdiction for education in each province. Under the terms of the same Act, the Federal Government is excluded from direct responsibility. In accordance with these terms each provincial legislature has organized a Department of Education administered by a Minister of Education assisted by a Deputy Minister who is a permanent civil servant. The typical Department of Education will have a Registrar to administer all of the records the Department must keep; directors to administer elementary education, secondary education, curriculum, audio-visual education, research, community and adult services, supervision and inspection, and building and planning. These Departments of Education are responsible for the administration of all the elementary and secondary schools in their respective provinces, and may, if arrangements are satisfactory, help supervise separate and private schools as well. For the most part the personnel to be found in Departments of Education are teachers, principals and superintendents who have chosen to become a part of the administrative system of the province.

PROVINCIAL

The Minister of Education in each province is the only minister in the provincial cabinet who does not have a counterpart in the Federal Cabinet. Whereas every other minister in a provincial cabinet may find his decisions tempered or modified by a federal minister who has overriding jurisdiction, such is not the case in education. The result of this situation has been a serious lack of federal perspective on education and an even more serious neglect of the kind of planning which only a federal agency can undertake. To a very minor extent several national professional bodies have attempted to provide the kind of overall planning that is needed, but because this kind of planning can only be partial at best it does not make up for the real loss. However, the Canadian Education Association, the Canadian Teachers' Federation, the Canadian Trustees Association, the Canadian Association of University Teachers, are organizations which bring together representative educational opinion from different parts of Canada, and though some of these opinions are at times quite disparate, the basis for a federal view is nonetheless there.

Recently the Council of Ministers of the Canadian Education Association has been, despite provincial biases, manifesting greater sensitivity to national needs. Thus the Council of Ministers has given support to a Canadian Council for Research in Education, to the National Home and School and Parent–Teacher Associations, to international educational programmes of action through the Department of External Affairs, and to national conferences on education. In spite of these efforts, however, the pattern of provincial control of education remains and militates against any really sound national development. The emergence of the Canadian Association of Universities and Colleges to help institutions of higher education meet the challenge of a much greater demand for their services is illustrative of the kind of demand for which the individual provinces are ill-prepared. The Canadian Association of Universities and Colleges very early in its development directed its attention to the Federal Cabinet pointing up the national need for trained personnel, and did so without in any way coming into conflict with provincial jurisdiction. In most instances, provincial governments have welcomed federal financial support for special and higher education.

LARGER UNITS

Each provincial educational system is divided into a number of administrative units. Originally these units were school districts four by five miles in area, but following the general increase in population across the country, it became evident that many of these school districts were too small for efficient administration. The advantages of having two or more districts co-operate in the operation of schools led to the discovery that there were further advantages to having several schools co-operate and ultimately to the development of larger units of administration made up of twenty or more school districts, depending upon geography and density of population. Quebec has been the most recent province to adopt the larger unit of administration which, according to "Project 55" will have fifty-five larger units in the entire province providing for a total population of approximately six million people. Exceptions to this pattern of larger units are to be found in Newfoundland and Ontario where, because of history and the development of denominational patterns units of administration are related to county forms and municipal boundaries.

The structures of the provincial educational systems are best seen in the set of diagrams recently prepared by the Education Division of the Dominion Bureau of Statistics. Though there are minor variations in the pattern of schools available in each province, in general the systems provide for elementary, secondary and higher educational institutions in both the private and public sectors. Vocational, technical, technological, adult and continuation programmes of various kinds are generally found in the public systems only primarily because of the costliness of these programmes.

Significant differences in the general pattern are to be found in the Newfoundland system where elementary and secondary schools are administered by five separate denominational boards; in the Quebec system where the proposed reorganization premises composite and higher educational institutions of a radically different order from those which obtained before; and in the Western Provinces where junior and community colleges have developed to an extent not seen elsewhere in Canada except Ontario but remarkably similar to patterns developed in the United States.

TRUSTEES

Each school district or unit is administered by a board of trustees who are usually elected for periods of from one to three years. These trustees are responsible to the Minister of Education for the administration of the provincial School Act in the district; their administration normally covers such matters as employment of the teacher or teachers; maintenance of the school premises; financial administration; and general supervision of policies. Where a district has several schools it may employ a school superintendent who will be the chief executive officer of the board and may or may not be responsible to the Department of Education as well as the board. The trustees of the provinces are generally organized into provincial associations and can and do exert considerable political pressures upon the provincial governments. These provincial trustees associations are still further organized into the Canadian School Trustees Association

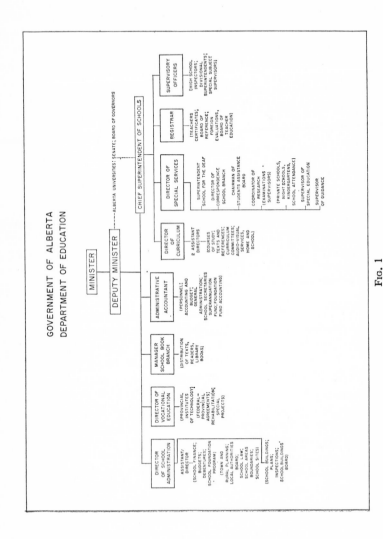

GOVERNMENT OF ALBERTA
DEPARTMENT OF EDUCATION

MINISTER

DEPUTY MINISTER

ALBERTA UNIVERSITIES; SENATE; BOARD OF GOVERNORS

CHIEF SUPERINTENDENT OF SCHOOLS

DIRECTOR OF SCHOOL ADMINISTRATION
ASSISTANT/ DIRECTOR
(SCHOOL FINANCE; BUDGETS; DEBENTURES; SCHOOL FOUNDATION PROGRAM)
(TOWN AND RURAL PLANNING; LOCAL AUTHORITIES BOARD; SCHOOL LAW; SCHOOL AREAS BOUNDARIES; SCHOOL SITES)
(SCHOOL BUILDINGS; PLANS; INSPECTIONS; SCHOOL BUILDINGS BOARD)

DIRECTOR OF VOCATIONAL EDUCATION
(PROVINCIAL INSTITUTES OF TECHNOLOGY)
(FEDERAL— PROVINCIAL AGREEMENTS; REHABILITATION; SPECIAL PROJECTS)

MANAGER SCHOOL BOOK BRANCH
(DISTRIBUTION OF TEXTS, READERS, LIBRARY BOOKS)

ADMINISTRATIVE ACCOUNTANT
(PERSONNEL; ACCOUNTING AND BUDGET; GENERAL ADMINISTRATION; SCHOOL SECRETARIES SUPERANNUATION FUND; FOUNDATION FUND ACCOUNTING)

DIRECTOR OF CURRICULUM
2 ASSISTANT DIRECTORS
(COURSES OF STUDY; TEXTS AND REFERENCES; CURRICULUM COMMITTEES; AUDIO-VISUAL SERVICES; HOME AND SCHOOL)

DIRECTOR OF SPECIAL SERVICES
SUPERINTENDENT SCHOOL FOR THE DEAF
DIRECTOR OF CORRESPONDENCE SCHOOL BRANCH
CHAIRMAN OF STUDENT'S ASSISTANCE BOARD
COORDINATOR OF RESEARCH
EXAMINATIONS SUPERVISORS
(PRIVATE SCHOOLS, NIGHT SCHOOLS, KINDERGARTENS, SCHOOL ATTENDANCE)
SUPERVISOR OF SPECIAL EDUCATION
SUPERVISOR OF GUIDANCE

REGISTRAR
(TEACHERS CERTIFICATES; BOARD OF REFERENCE; FOREIGN EVALUATIONS; BOARD OF TEACHER EDUCATION)

SUPERVISORY OFFICERS
(HIGH SCHOOL INSPECTORS; DIVISIONAL SUPERINTENDENTS; SPECIAL SUBJECT SUPERVISORS)

Fig. 1

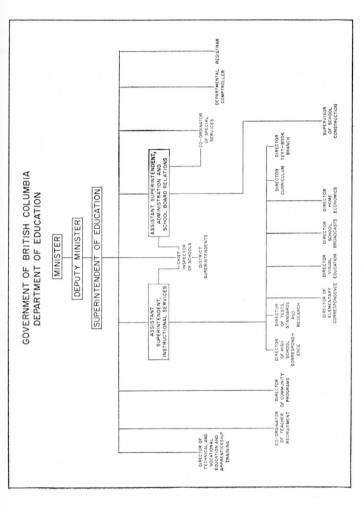

GOVERNMENT OF BRITISH COLUMBIA
DEPARTMENT OF EDUCATION

MINISTER

DEPUTY MINISTER

SUPERINTENDENT OF EDUCATION

ASSISTANT SUPERINTENDENT, INSTRUCTIONAL SERVICES

ASSISTANT SUPERINTENDENT, ADMINISTRATION AND SCHOOL BOARD RELATIONS

CHIEF INSPECTOR OF SCHOOLS

DISTRICT SUPERINTENDENTS

CO-ORDINATOR OF SPECIAL SERVICES

DEPARTMENTAL COMPTROLLER

DEPARTMENTAL REGISTRAR

DIRECTOR OF TECHNICAL AND VOCATIONAL EDUCATION AND APPRENTICESHIP TRAINING

CO-ORDINATOR OF TEACHER RECRUITMENT

DIRECTOR OF COMMUNITY PROGRAMS

DIRECTOR OF HIGH SCHOOL CORRESPONDENCE

DIRECTOR OF TESTS, STANDARDS AND RESEARCH

DIRECTOR OF ELEMENTARY CORRESPONDENCE EDUCATION

DIRECTOR VISUAL EDUCATION

DIRECTOR SCHOOL BROADCASTS

DIRECTOR HOME ECONOMICS

DIRECTOR CURRICULUM

DIRECTOR TEXT-BOOK BRANCH

SUPERVISOR OF SCHOOL CONSTRUCTION

FIG. 2

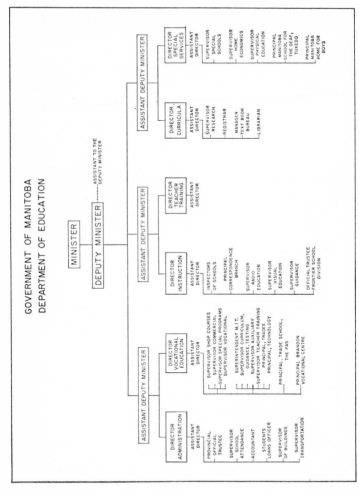

FIG. 3

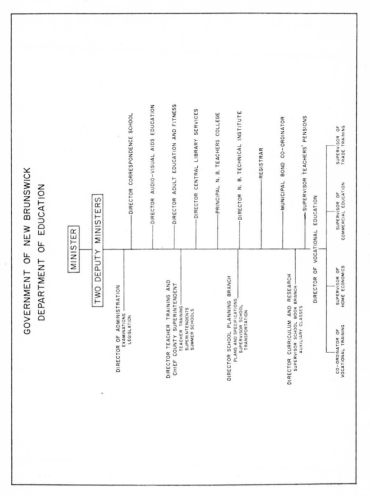

GOVERNMENT OF NEW BRUNSWICK
DEPARTMENT OF EDUCATION

MINISTER

TWO DEPUTY MINISTERS

DIRECTOR OF ADMINISTRATION
  EXAMINATIONS
  LEGISLATION

DIRECTOR CORRESPONDENCE SCHOOL

DIRECTOR AUDIO-VISUAL AIDS EDUCATION

DIRECTOR ADULT EDUCATION AND FITNESS

DIRECTOR CENTRAL LIBRARY SERVICES

DIRECTOR TEACHER TRAINING AND
CHIEF COUNTY SUPERINTENDENT
  TEACHER TRAINING
  SUPERINTENDENTS
  SUMMER SCHOOLS

PRINCIPAL N. B. TEACHERS COLLEGE

DIRECTOR N. B. TECHNICAL INSTITUTE

DIRECTOR SCHOOL PLANNING BRANCH
  PLANS AND SPECIFICATIONS
  SUPERVISOR SCHOOL
  TRANSPORTATION

REGISTRAR

MUNICIPAL BOND CO-ORDINATOR

DIRECTOR CURRICULUM AND RESEARCH
  SUPERVISOR SCHOOL BOOK BRANCH
  AUXILIARY CLASSES

SUPERVISOR TEACHERS' PENSIONS

DIRECTOR OF VOCATIONAL EDUCATION

CO-ORDINATOR OF
VOCATIONAL TRAINING

SUPERVISOR OF
HOME ECONOMICS

SUPERVISOR OF
COMMERCIAL EDUCATION

SUPERVISOR OF
TRADE TRAINING

FIG. 4

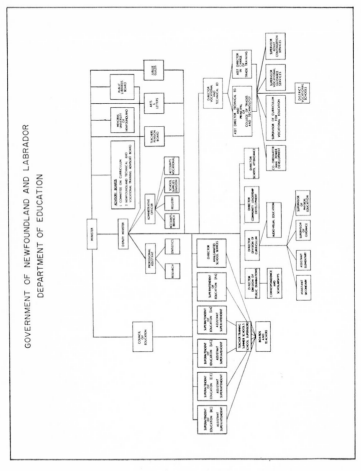

FIG. 5

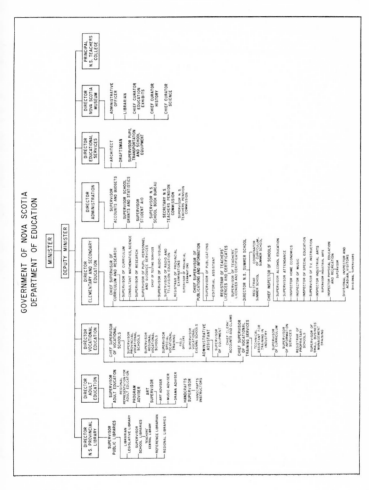

GOVERNMENT OF NOVA SCOTIA
DEPARTMENT OF EDUCATION

Fig. 6

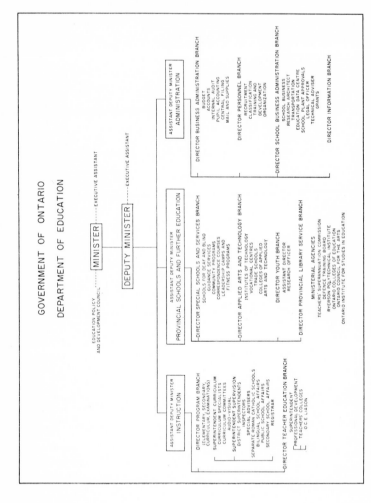

GOVERNMENT OF ONTARIO
DEPARTMENT OF EDUCATION

EDUCATION POLICY .... MINISTER ------ EXECUTIVE ASSISTANT
AND DEVELOPMENT COUNCIL

DEPUTY MINISTER ------ EXECUTIVE ASSISTANT

ASSISTANT DEPUTY MINISTER INSTRUCTION

DIRECTOR PROGRAM BRANCH
(ELEMENTARY, SECONDARY, CURRICULUM, EXAMINATIONS)
SUPERINTENDENT CURRICULUM
CURRICULUM SPECIALISTS
CURRICULUM COMMITTEES
AUDIO-VISUAL
SUPERINTENDENT SUPERVISION
DISTRICT SUPERINTENDENTS
INSPECTORS
SPECIAL ADVISERS
SEPARATE ROMAN CATHOLIC SCHOOLS
BILINGUAL SCHOOL AFFAIRS
PUBLIC SCHOOL AFFAIRS
SECONDARY SCHOOL AFFAIRS
REGISTRAR
DIRECTOR TEACHER EDUCATION BRANCH
SUPERINTENDENT
PROFESSIONAL DEVELOPMENT
TEACHERS' COLLEGES
O.C.E. LIAISON

ASSISTANT DEPUTY MINISTER PROVINCIAL SCHOOLS AND FURTHER EDUCATION

DIRECTOR SPECIAL SCHOOLS AND SERVICES BRANCH
SCHOOLS FOR DEAF AND BLIND
GUIDANCE SERVICES
COMMUNITY PROGRAMS
CORRESPONDENCE COURSES
LEADERSHIP CAMPS AND
FITNESS PROGRAMS
DIRECTOR APPLIED ARTS AND TECHNOLOGY BRANCH
INSTITUTES OF TECHNOLOGY
VOCATIONAL CENTRES
TRADE SCHOOLS
COLLEGES OF APPLIED
ARTS AND TECHNOLOGY
DIRECTOR YOUTH BRANCH
ASSISTANT DIRECTOR
RESEARCH OFFICER
DIRECTOR PROVINCIAL LIBRARY SERVICE BRANCH

MINISTERIAL AGENCIES
TEACHERS SUPERANNUATION COMMISSION
DEFENCE TRAINING BOARD
RYERSON POLYTECHNICAL INSTITUTE
ONTARIO COLLEGES OF EDUCATION
ONTARIO COUNCIL FOR THE ARTS
ONTARIO INSTITUTE FOR STUDIES IN EDUCATION

ASSISTANT DEPUTY MINISTER ADMINISTRATION

DIRECTOR BUSINESS ADMINISTRATION BRANCH
BUDGET
ACCOUNTS
INTERNAL AUDIT
PUPIL ACCOUNTING
CENTRAL FILING
MAIL AND SUPPLIES
DIRECTOR PERSONNEL BRANCH
RECRUITMENT
CLASSIFICATION
TRAINING AND
DEVELOPMENT
ORGANIZATION
DIRECTOR SCHOOL BUSINESS ADMINISTRATION BRANCH
SCHOOL BUSINESS
RESEARCH ARCHITECT
TRANSPORTATION
EDUCATION DATA CENTRE
SCHOOL PLANT APPROVALS
LEGAL OFFICER
TECHNICAL ADVISER
GRANTS
DIRECTOR INFORMATION BRANCH

FIG. 7

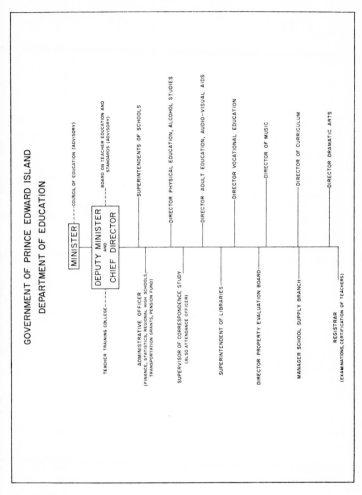

GOVERNMENT OF PRINCE EDWARD ISLAND
DEPARTMENT OF EDUCATION

MINISTER ----- COUNCIL OF EDUCATION (ADVISORY)

DEPUTY MINISTER AND CHIEF DIRECTOR ----- BOARD ON TEACHER EDUCATION AND STANDARDS (ADVISORY)

TEACHER TRAINING COLLEGE -----

ADMINISTRATIVE OFFICER (FINANCE, STATISTICS, REGIONAL HIGH SCHOOLS, TRANSPORTATION GRANTS, PENSION FUND)

SUPERVISOR OF CORRESPONDENCE STUDY (ALSO ATTENDANCE OFFICER)

SUPERINTENDENT OF LIBRARIES

DIRECTOR PROPERTY EVALUATION BOARD

MANAGER SCHOOL SUPPLY BRANCH

REGISTRAR (EXAMINATIONS, CERTIFICATION OF TEACHERS)

SUPERINTENDENTS OF SCHOOLS

DIRECTOR PHYSICAL EDUCATION, ALCOHOL STUDIES

DIRECTOR ADULT EDUCATION, AUDIO-VISUAL AIDS

DIRECTOR VOCATIONAL EDUCATION

DIRECTOR OF MUSIC

DIRECTOR OF CURRICULUM

DIRECTOR DRAMATIC ARTS

Fig. 8

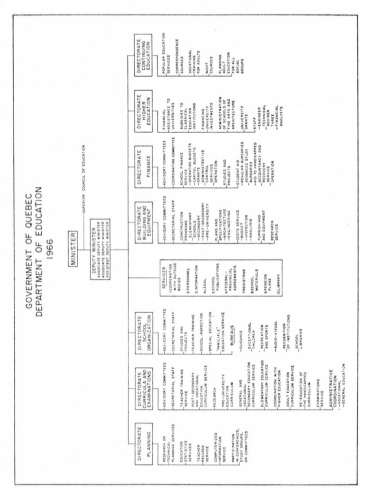

GOVERNMENT OF QUEBEC
DEPARTMENT OF EDUCATION
1966

Fig. 9

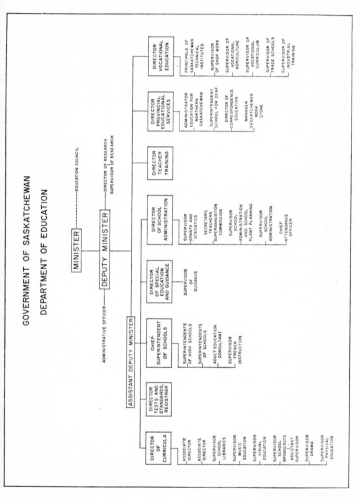

GOVERNMENT OF SASKATCHEWAN
DEPARTMENT OF EDUCATION

Fig. 10

and this body has from time to time exerted considerable political pressure at the Federal level and at the same time undertaken some very worthwhile studies into educational finance in Canadian education.

TEACHERS

The teachers for their part have their own provincial organizations banded together in the Canadian Teachers' Federation. Each provincial teachers' society acts as a professional body protecting the interests of its members and ensuring that each teacher has the resources of a professional organization in contracts with boards and departmental regulations. These teachers' organizations have over the years developed professional codes which all teachers are expected to adhere to; helped raise salaries and ensured equitable financial returns for improved professional services. The provincial teachers' associations in co-operation with the national federation have been engaging in more research and study than has been the case heretofore. Studies in teacher education, finance, overseas service, curriculum and report cards have been among some of the interests of these organizations. Departments of Education have found it increasingly important to consult with members of the teachers' federations on many educational policies. Nevertheless, and despite the growing professionalism of the teachers' associations, the ultimate responsibility for the conduct of the educational system rests with the Minister of Education who in turn is responsible to the provincial cabinet and in turn to the legislature. In consequence of this line of responsibility the teaching profession in all parts of Canada is politically sensitive and vulnerable.

Teachers' associations have for years wanted to share with Departments of Education the authority to certify teachers and thus ensure that in times of teacher shortage expedient measures would not be introduced in order to keep classrooms open with people not at all qualified to teach or at best only partially trained. However, the best the teachers have been able to gain in some provinces is a representative or two on professional boards of schools and Departments of Education without any special responsibility beyond this. This desire to achieve a measure of control of teacher certification constitutes one of the goals of the teaching profession. This goal is being tangentially achieved by way of the schools of education in universities where standards for the academic performance of secondary school teachers in training are beyond the direct influence of any certifying body. In consequence, where elementary teachers are trained in normal schools and teachers colleges outside the influence of a university there is a sufficient disparity in requirements to raise a question of public and professional confidence in the preparation of elementary teachers outside the university or Junior Colleges when these develop such programs.

PARENT–TEACHERS

Home and School and Parent–Teacher Associations are to be found in each of the provinces and these, like teachers and trustees, are organized federally. Parent–teacher associations have generally enjoyed their most successful experiences in elementary schools where parental enthusiasms have been accommodated by enthusiastic teachers. On the other hand, parent–teacher associations have not been as successful in secondary schools. In the main, parents of secondary school students have learned to accept their roles as partial observers and because of this are not as enthusiastic about home and school associations. The secondary school student for his part is somewhat less than enthusiastic about having his parents and his teachers confer regularly about his progress or lack of it. Home and school and parent–teacher associations have, however, helped many a secondary and elementary school to acquire audio-visual equipment, furniture, books and materials. These associations have been able to bring considerable pressure to bear at both provincial and federal levels on matters of educational finance, of health and physical education, on the education of the physically handicapped, and upon counselling and guidance. In many ways home and school associations have seemed to pressure school boards and legislatures to adopt programmes and policies which otherwise might well have been neglected or entirely overlooked.

FEDERAL GOVERNMENT

Although the British North America Act stipulated that education was to be exclusively a provincial matter, the Federal Government has nonetheless been called upon to devote more attention and monies to education at all levels. In 1913 the Federal Government passed the Agricultural Instruction Act and appropriated $10,000,000 to implement its provisions. In 1919 the Technical Education Act was passed, and in 1939 the Youth Training Act followed in 1942 by the Vocational Training Coordination Act. Following the Second World War the Canada Council was established for the purpose of supporting and developing the arts, letters and sciences in Canada, and the Social Science Research Council to further research in these areas. In this period, too, the Federal Government began to supply funds for higher education and in 1966 raised the federal contribution from $2·00 to $5·00 *per capita*. All provinces except Quebec have been appreciative if not happy with federal help to education and have used the funds to good advantage. Quebec has preferred to offer its own aid to universities even though equivalent funds need to be transferred from the federal to the provincial treasury.

Federal funds find their way into a wide variety of educational programmes not all of which are identified with schools, colleges or universities but which, nonetheless, help both youth and adults to a better and more understanding way of life. Thus, the training programmes of the Department of National Defence, the Officers' Training Corps, and the Vocational Training Branch of the Department of Labour are federally financed; the publications of the Dominion Bureau of Statistics as well as those of the Queen's Printer find their way into private, public and school libraries and community agencies. The Family Allowances Act has provided federal funds for all children from birth to 16 years of age to ensure minimum standards of health, food and clothing. A survey of the results of this programme soon showed that there was improved attendance and performance at school on the part of many children. National physical fitness programmes, cadet programmes, and educational programmes for penitentiaries have all been financed by federal funds and agencies without too serious complaints by provincial governments and organizations. The Canadian Broadcasting Corporation, a federal crown corporation responsible for maintaining national networks for radio and TV, spends large sums of money each year on educational programmes, many of which are supervised and locally administered by provincial agencies. Federal and provincial agencies cooperate in almost all of these programmes, many of which are regionally oriented. Most recently the Economic Council of Canada, a federal agency, has been looking closely at the productivity of the Canadian educational systems as this productivity bears upon the industrial and economic potential of the country. In all probability federal interest in education will move from the informal to the formal category before many years.

MUNICIPALITIES

Although municipal governments, city, town, village or county each have one or more school boards to administer the local educational system or systems, the councils of these municipal bodies are in the last resort responsible for collecting the local taxes needed to maintain the schools within their respective boundaries. From time to time differences between councils and school boards arise, but these are generally settled before arbitration boards are called upon, as they may be, to settle any disputes. Departments of Education and Departments of Municipal Affairs in provincial administrations generally have regulations which more or less lay down the guidelines of operation of both councils and school boards.

Private schools are also to be found in all provinces of Canada, though the largest number are located in Quebec and Ontario. For the most part these private schools select their student bodies from the upper middle class whose incomes are sufficient to maintain one or more children in fairly expensive establishments. In general, private schools are looked upon by the general public as a symbol of class conscious ambitions not in line with the North American ethos. Private schools are also considered to be élitist in their outlook as distinct from the mass education approach of the public schools and for this reason are not generally acceptable. Nevertheless, private schools do exist to meet the needs of children whose parents can afford the special attention required. In addition, there are the private commercial schools, language schools, art schools, and technical schools for that sector of the population able to pay for services and attentions the public sector cannot provide.

DENOMINATIONAL SCHOOLS

The private school sector of Canada is extensive and varied. As of 1959 there were in Canada some 950 private academic elementary and secondary schools: 37 in the Atlantic Provinces, 604 in Quebec, 114 in Ontario, 126 in the Prairie Provinces, 69 in British Columbia. These schools employed about 7500 teachers and enrolled over 130,000 students, a little less than 4 per cent of public school enrolment. Private schools, denominational or non-sectarian, may or may not be subsidized out of public funds. Denominations represented are primarily Catholic, but there are Anglican, Seventh Day Adventist, Hebrew, Protestant, United Church, Greek Catholic, Church of God, Christian Reformed, Lutheran, Baptist, Hutterite, Chinese, and non-sectarian. These schools may be day or residential schools, range from kindergarten through Grade 13, be taught in French, English, in some instances, German, Hebrew, Chinese, and Ukrainian. Most are coeducational, but there are those, primarily residential, that cater to either boys or girls.

Most provinces of Canada make some kind of arrangement to

share public funds with separate or denominational schools. However, British Columbia makes no such provision, and Manitoba provides only shared technical services. The province of Quebec has been the only one to give Catholic and Protestant schools a proportionate share of the province's educational dollar. The question of public funds for sectarian education has been a problem in Canada ever since the schools first established by the missionaries and the religious orders began to be taken over by the provincial governments. The most contentious debate on this problem took place in connection with the Manitoba School Question in 1905, when the provincial government passed legislation denying public funds to Catholic schools that had been established prior to the entry of Manitoba into Confederation, and had enjoyed public support until that time. Fortunately, or unfortunately, the MacFarlane Report reopened the entire question in 1959 without providing any real guidelines to an amicable solution.

MILITARY SCHOOLS

The Department of National Defence maintains a system of schools for the children of overseas personnel in Europe. In addition, this Department maintains three service colleges providing balanced arts, science and military training leading to degrees. These service colleges are the Royal Military College of Canada at Kingston, Ontario; Royal Roads at Victoria, B.C.; and College Militaire Royal de Saint-Jean established at St. Jean, Quebec. In addition there are the Royal Canadian Air Force College at Armour Heights in Toronto; the Royal Officers Training Corps to be found in the universities; and the Cadets Corps to be found in selected secondary schools across the country.

The Federal Government maintains schools in Europe for the children of personnel in the Armed Forces. These schools are located at Marville in France, at Zweibrucken and Baden-Soellinger in West Germany, and at Cagliari, Sardinia. These schools follow a programme based on the courses in Canadian schools especially arranged so as to make it possible for students to transfer to any school in Canada on return. Teachers for these schools are recruited from school systems in Canada, as are the administrative personnel. Teachers and principals may serve only for a period of two years with option to repeat for one year.

In 1965 there were about 5200 children in Europe with 700 of these in Metz. Student population tends to be highest in the lower grades because of the relative youth of the service personnel. School enrolment in Grades 1, 2 and 3 totals 1828 in comparison with 420 in the senior high school grades. Because servicemen are required to move about from post to post, children are frequently required to attend make-up classes in order to bring them up to standard in some subject areas. On the other hand, many of these students have the advantage of superior studies in geography, history, art, music and languages as a result of academic and general cultural classes and tours.

CHAPTER 5

Primary and Elementary Schools

GENERAL

Canadian primary and elementary schools are, for the most part, publicly controlled, or administered by private agencies. Schools for native Indians and Eskimos are operated by the Federal Government, as are schools for overseas personnel in Europe. There are approximately three and a half million child ren in these schools ranging in age from 5 to 12 years. In some instances there may be nursery or kindergarten classes for children 3 years of age and over, attached to the regular elementary school but these still constitute a minority.

In the main these schools are housed in fine buildings and are well equipped for both study and play. Classrooms are light and airy, very well furnished and equipped; gymnasia and auditoria adequate; and where justified by the size of the school population and supported by the local budget science laboratories, libraries, home economics, and vocational educational facilities may be provided. Not all Canadian communities are able to afford elaborately equipped and housed elementary schools. Communities in rural areas, or in those less well-endowed with natural resources such as the Atlantic Provinces, Manitoba, or the northern areas of most provinces can only afford the minimum necessary. This minimum provision, however, will still ensure each child a basic educational programme.

Enrolment in public elementary schools in the year 1965–6 from kindergarten through Grade 8 was of the order of 3,619,126 pupils; in private schools pupils numbered 110,141; and in federal schools, there were 31,378 Indian and Eskimo children.

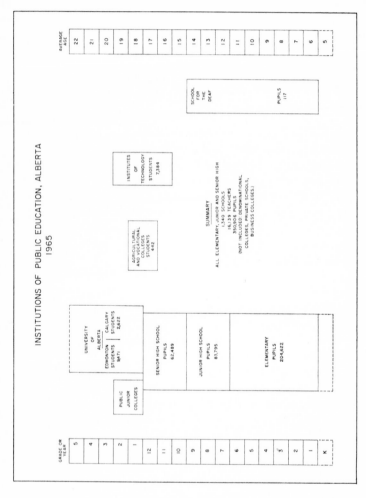

FIG. 11

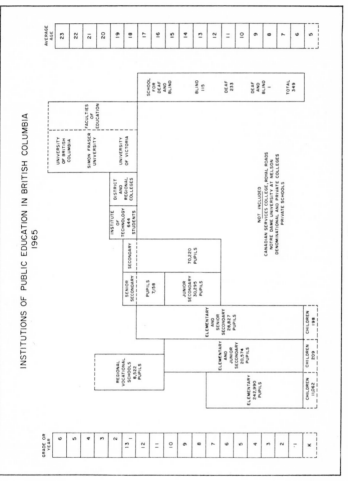

INSTITUTIONS OF PUBLIC EDUCATION IN BRITISH COLUMBIA
1965

Fig. 12

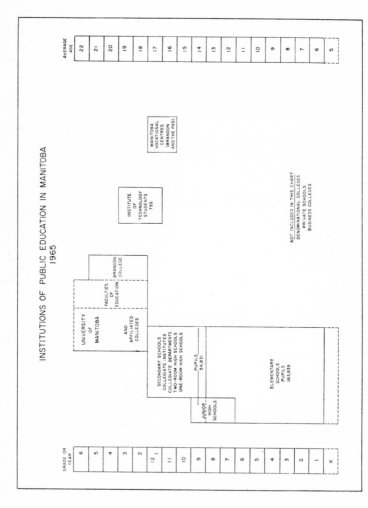

Fig. 13

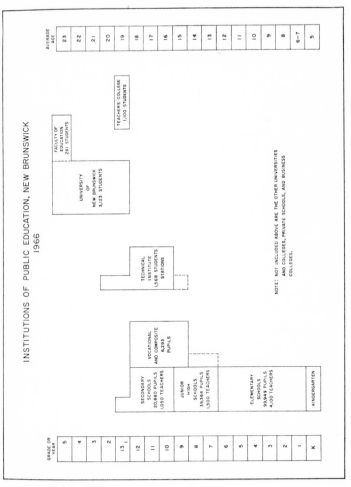

FIG. 14

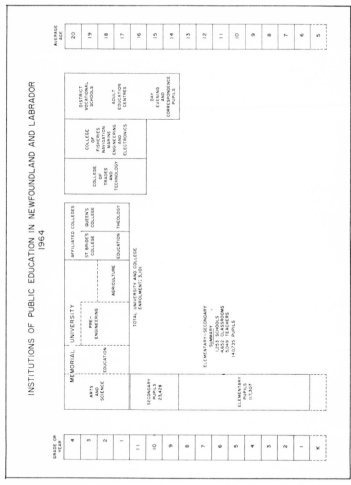

INSTITUTIONS OF PUBLIC EDUCATION IN NEWFOUNDLAND AND LABRADOR
1964

Fig. 15

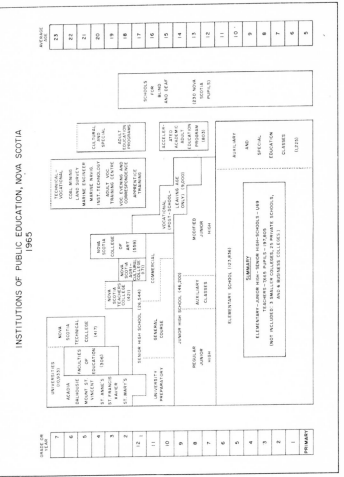

INSTITUTIONS OF PUBLIC EDUCATION, NOVA SCOTIA 1965

Fig. 16

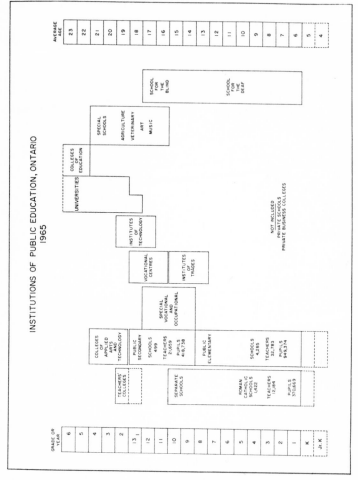

Fig. 17

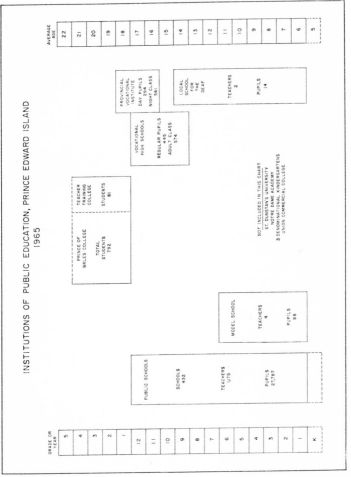

INSTITUTIONS OF PUBLIC EDUCATION, PRINCE EDWARD ISLAND
1965

AVERAGE AGE
22
21
20
19
18
17
16
15
14
13
12
11
10
9
8
7
6
5

PROVINCIAL VOCATIONAL INSTITUTE
DAY PUPILS 294
NIGHT CLASS 561

VOCATIONAL HIGH SCHOOLS
REGULAR PUPILS 445
ADULT CLASS 574

LOCAL SCHOOL FOR THE DEAF
TEACHERS 2
PUPILS 14

TEACHER TRAINING COLLEGE
PRINCE OF WALES COLLEGE
TOTAL STUDENTS 792
STUDENTS 81

NOT INCLUDED IN THIS CHART
ST. DUNSTAN'S UNIVERSITY
NOTRE DAME ACADEMY
3 DENOMINATIONAL KINDERGARTENS
UNION COMMERCIAL COLLEGE

MODEL SCHOOL
TEACHERS 4
PUPILS 88

PUBLIC SCHOOLS
SCHOOLS 432
TEACHERS 1,175
PUPILS 27,787

GRADE OR YEAR
5
4
3
2
1
12
11
10
9
8
7
6
5
4
3
2
1
K

Fig. 18

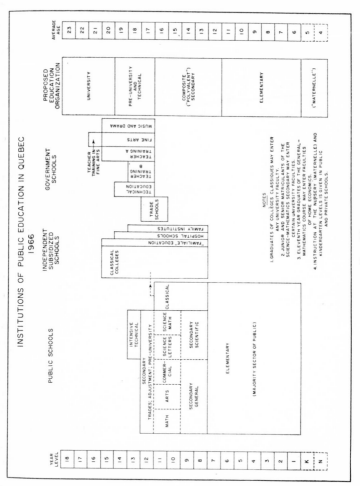

Fig. 19

Primary and Elementary Schools

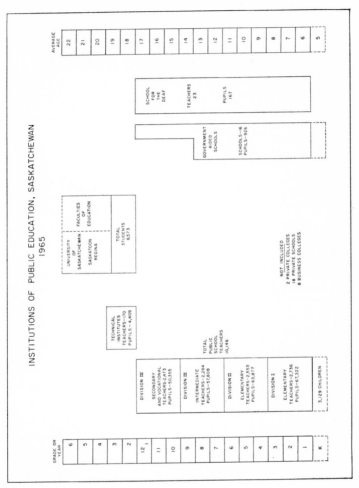

INSTITUTIONS OF PUBLIC EDUCATION, SASKATCHEWAN
1965

Fig. 20

Society, Schools and Progress in Canada

These figures must be read in the context of a total population in Canada of about 20,000,000 people and a total elementary and secondary school population of approximately five million.

HISTORY

Among the earliest schools in Canada were those operated by the Jesuits in 1635 for French and Indian children. In 1735 the Sisters of Congregation opened their first school in Nova Scotia at Louisburg, and in 1749 the Society for the Promotion of the Gospel in Foreign Parts sent a schoolmaster to Nova Scotia. In the main, these early elementary schools offered reading, writing and catechism as the academic fare. Between 1750 and 1815 elementary education in Canada was sponsored by private and religious bodies. Between 1815 and 1845 some state assistance was provided to local settlers who organized elementary school programmes. In many instances these locally sponsored programmes were dependent upon itinerant teachers not all of whom were either capable or fit for the responsibilities of the job. In the period 1845–75 a more or less uniform standard of elementary education under the control of municipal and provincial authorities came into being. By 1875 most elementary schools in Eastern Canada at least had been brought to a uniform standard under central authorities. Following this period of centralization Canadian elementary schools came increasingly under the influence of American educational thinking, and particularly under the influence of schools of thought which had their origin in Europe and in Britain. In the last half of the nineteenth century Canadian elementary practices were shaped by principles of education set forth by Pestalozzi, by Herbert and by Froebel. Egerton Ryerson, the first Superintendent of Education in Ontario, was largely instrumental in bringing these ideas to bear upon Canadian education.

Elementary education was initially influenced by the work of the Ursuline Sisters, by the Jesuits, and by those who operated charity, monitorial, Sunday and infant schools. Many of these early schools were staffed by people whose qualifications were characterized more by love than by learning with the result that in all too many instances the students were too ill prepared for advancement in further study. Nonetheless, these schools laid the basis for a general attitude toward education in the community which enabled schools to remain open to children for increasingly longer periods. According to Phillips the average number of months of schooling achieved by children increased from 5 to 90 in 120 years:

1830	1850	1870	1890	1910	1930	1950
5	10	30	35	55	80	90

Since then this figure of 90 has again increased to 100.

In the 1950's of every 1000 pupils who entered grade one there were 940 who continued through to Grade 5 and about 700 who completed Grade 8. In the twenty years between 1930 and 1950 there had been a net gain of 200 pupils who continued their elementary education through to the end of Grade 8. The holding power of the schools is excellent for all provinces in Canada up to and including Grade 6, after which the drop-out rate increases, particularly among rural, native and economically and socially depressed populations in urban centres.

ADMINISTRATION

The responsibility for the organization and administration of the elementary school programme rests with the principal, subject to the approval of the superintendent and supervisors who have overall responsibility for several schools in an urban or rural area. The principal as the senior official in the school is responsible for interpreting school board policy to teachers and parents and for ensuring that all policies and programmes in the school are conducted in accordance with school law. The elementary school principal's task is considered particularly important in respect to explaining the school's programme to parents whose young children are just beginning their school careers. The home and school and parent–teacher associations are usually very active in elementary schools and these organizations are often very helpful to a particular school in providing needed equipment and in giving the school much needed support for programmes not normally financed by regular school budgets. Principals and teachers usually work well together with the executives of these associations.

Principals, teachers and supervisors place a good deal of emphasis upon good health and physical education programmes in the school and arrange for regular schedules of athletic and game activities. In addition to this attention to the physical well-being of the child many school systems, particularly those located in urban centres, provide child guidance clinics where child psychologists, speech therapists, psychometrists, medical doctors and psychiatrists make up teams to treat those children who manifest deviant or aberrant behaviour characteristics. In some centres classes or school programmes are provided for the physically handicapped, the emotionally and the socially disturbed. In several cases mental health programmes form part of the regular school offerings.

The elementary school child usually begins his school day at 9 o'clock and continues through to 3, 3:30 or 4 o'clock depending upon the arrangement of the school programme. The morning session, which usually lasts until 12 o'clock noon, generally provides for a 15 minute recess, a provision which is also made in the afternoon. Children attending kindergarten are usually expected to attend only a morning or afternoon session but not both, an arrangement which is suitable for 5-year olds, and one which also makes it possible for the school to serve twice as many children as it normally would. By the time a child has attended a five-day school week for forty weeks during the year he is generally ready for the summer vacation in July and August. During the course of the school year the child also enjoys ten days' vacation at both Christmas and Easter, and as well such additional religious holy days as his ethnic or religious background allow.

CURRICULUM

The original elementary school programme of reading, writing, arithmetic, religion, needlework and cooking changed radically over the years. In the years following 1850 there were added grammar and geography, and after 1895 literature, history, music and drawing. After 1900 courses of study were again modified with the addition of nature study, art, manual training and household science.

More important than the addition of specific courses of study, however, was the adoption of a general philosophy of elementary education which made it possible to see the child as an individual human being possessed of characteristics peculiar to particular stages of development and not as a mere small replica of an adult. The changes in the philosophy of the elementary school have been influenced by the writings of child study specialists, by the findings of child development studies, and by the research contributions of psychologists, psychiatrists, and anthropologists all of whom have provided new perspectives on the nature of childhood.

The curriculum of the elementary school is affected by the pattern of grade organization obtaining in the school system in which the elementary school is located. Since there are a variety of school organizational patterns, e.g. 8–4; 3–3–6; 3–3–3–3, 6–3–3; 3–3–3–4; and 7–4–4; children may proceed from grade to grade in a variety of ways. Because of the different patterns to be found there are also different promotion policies with the result that group performances in any one grade vary across the country.

More recently elementary schools have been experimenting with non-graded classes with a view to helping children advance at their own rates and avoid the frustration of lock-step promotion. The results of these early experiments have proved to be sufficiently good to warrant wider adoption of the practice. At the same time, these schools have also adopted the practice of having several teachers made available to each class giving the children the benefit of being taught by subject specialists. Although teachers of music, art and physical education were generally available to the elementary grades, the specialist approach has, in some cases, been extended to mathematics, science, and languages.

A large portion of the time of the primary school child is devoted to learning to read, write and do arithmetic. Although the central purpose of this early schooling is held to be the development of intellectual skills, a good deal of importance is attached to the social development of the individual. For this reason there are in the elementary school large blocks of time allocated to group activities on the playground as well as in the school. The child is also given many opportunities for free expression in and out of group activities.

A typical elementary school schedule showing grades, subjects, and minutes per week devoted to each is shown in the accompanying table. The child graduating from a programme of this kind will be prepared to advance toward further studies in the junior secondary school, but will not be in a position to leave school for any good position in industry; in brief, the elementary school programme is designed to prepare children for further schooling or, at best, for further training on the job.

PROGRAMMES

Reading continues to be the subject of central concern in the elementary school. Low levels of achievement in reading have led to experimentation with a wide variety of methods including the much publicized augmented alphabet promoted by Pitman. The debate concerning the look-and-say method versus the phonetic method continues to engage public and professional alike, but for the most part the school authorities have settled on a mixture of both. On the whole, the place accorded developmental reading programmes in elementary schools is entirely respectable, though the same may not be said for remedial programmes for this field. Many school systems, particularly those in urban centres, provide clinical services for children having physiological or emotional reading problems, and these have for the most part justified their

An Elementary School Schedule

Grades — Subjects	1	2	3	4	5	6
Health	60*	60	60	60	60	60
Games and Exercises	80	80	100	100	100	100
Reading, Phonics Library	500	450	375	300	200	200
Language: Oral	65	65	80	80	80	80
Written	60	60	80	80	80	80
Speech	—	80	120	120	100	100
Writing	50	50	75	75	60	60
Spelling	—	70	120	120	100	100
French			150	150	150	150
Arithmetic	100	100	150	200	200	200
Social Studies	45	45	50	70	200	200
Enterprise†	150	150	150	150	150	150
Science and Nature Study	30	30	50	60	60	60
Music	75	75	75	75	60	60
Art	60	60	60	60	75	75
Practical Arts	60	60	60	60	75	75
Morals and‡ Religion				30—150		150
Play	150	150	150	150	150	150

Grades — Subjects	7	8
Health	200	200
Physical Exercise		
Library	40	40
English: Grammar, Spelling, Literature, Composition	200	280
Social Studies: History	240	240
Geography	200	200
Civics		
Science	120	120
Art	80	160
Industrial Arts	80	160
Home Economics	80—160	
Agriculture		80
Typing		80
Study		80

* Minutes per week.   † Alberta and Saskatchewan.   ‡ Quebec mainly.

existence. In some provinces, these clinical services are also made available to rural children.

For the most part the authors of primers and elementary school readers have presented Canadian children with a diet of sentences and stories which have been characterized by a signal lack of intellectual challenge. Many elementary school children today in Canada are saved from entire intellectual boredom by increased attendance at public libraries which generally have a wide selection of books for all age groups, and by watching some of the worthwhile television programmes especially prepared for children. Departments of Audio-Visual Instruction have been developing programmes of special interest for young children and these are for the most part stimulating, informative and challenging. To a very considerable extent it is the practice in elementary schools to relate the reading in one subject area to that done in another so that there is constant reinforcement of the particular learning experience.

In addition to reading, writing and arithmetic continue to be given the traditional emphasis in the programme. The social studies are given much more attention than formerly with geography, history and civics the main subject offered. Games and physical exercises play an important part in all phases of the elementary programme and these are generally integrated with studies in health education and with music, dancing and art. Oral and written language, the study of printing and script, the creation of poems and plays, all constitute an integral part of the education of the young child. In those school systems where Grades 7 and 8 form part of the elementary system, the study of home economics by girls and of industrial arts by boys is made possible. In rural schools the care of garden plots allied to the study of agriculture is also included in the programme. More and more schools, too, are providing opportunities for students to learn typing, sometimes in connection with a commercial course, but quite often apart from it.

The emphasis upon science in the general curriculum has also had its effect upon the programme of the elementary school.

Though general science is given priority, in some instances attention is paid to the separate fields of science, physics, chemistry, biology, botany, zoology and astronomy. In urban areas where children have ready access to television programmes their knowledge of science even at the elementary school level is relatively sophisticated with the result that urban school science programmes have to be sufficiently comprehensive and imaginative to warrant the interest of the student who has television offerings as a criterion. Where the urban child has the advantage of television, the rural child has the benefit of being closer to field and stream and in consequence has readier access to nature walks and close observation.

THE GIFTED

Special classes for students who have better than average ability have been adopted by several school systems. In general, these major work classes begin in Grade 4 and continue through to Grade 8. In addition to the general work of the grade, students are given a wider variety of tasks calling for more advanced skills and greater depth and breadth of insight. Where students manifest exceptional ability some systems permit the skipping of one grade, but this practice is not encouraged since the student may encounter later difficulties as a result of having missed some basic work. Major work classes generally call for a specially selected teacher capable of meeting the challenges of extremely active and alert groups.

CREATIVE CLASSES

In art and music a special effort is made to free students from too rigid requirements in order to foster the creative powers of the children. While the regular programme may call for three or four hours of art and music each week in each grade, there are many additional opportunities for art and music in connection with special events and days throughout the year and teachers and children are encouraged to take advantage of these. The religious and secular holidays provide many occasions for children in art and music classes to display their powers of creativity and advantage is taken of this fact. When possible concerts and public showings are arranged so that parents and public alike may be given an opportunity to witness the productivity of the children.

POVERTY PROGRAMMES

Because the affluent society does not reach all sectors of the community many children in school do not have the advantages of homes which provide them with the minimum of books, guides and references, and study places needed. In consequence special attention is given to children in low socio-economic areas by adapting the educational programmes to their special needs and by providing them with the additional resources and training required. Again, special programmes have to be prepared to acquaint teachers with the attitudes and customs of this sector of the school population in several respects quite different from those of their regular students. These disadvantaged children are found in both rural and urban communities but for the most part in urban where populations in transition are more likely to be found.

DISCIPLINE

Corporal punishment may be administered by a teacher or principal in most school systems in Canada, but such punishment must be administered in accordance with school law and be reasonable. In general such punishment takes the form of strokes with a leather or rubber strap applied to the hand of the child or student, and so applied that no permanent injury may result. Strapping as such must be witnessed by a member of staff, in the case of a principal applying the punishment, and in some provinces, the strapping must be reported upon in writing to the school board. Physical punishment is not generally approved, the educational psychologists adducing that a child may be reasoned with under all circumstances and on all occasions, and the personnel counsellors suggesting that an adequate assessment of all the relevant factors will always eschew physical punishment. However, parents, teachers, and educators, though recognizing that physical punishment as such is not the final answer, nor by any means the best, still believe that where there is a wide spectrum of socio-ethical values in any single classroom a quick means of discipline is essential. The rules and regulations governing this conduct vary from one school act to another in Canada, but in the main, the provisions are generally similar.

PLAYGROUNDS

All primary and elementary schools have playgrounds of one kind or another. Play is considered to be an important part of the school curriculum, and both in-school and out-of-school activities provide opportunities for children to direct their energies in games of one kind and another.

The playgrounds surrounding elementary schools are generally covered by grass or cinders and arranged so as to make it convenient for both boys and girls to play football, baseball, handball, volleyball, and engage in a wide variety of athletics and individual games of skill. The regular schedule of activities in elementary schools provides time for games in class and gymnasia where these are available and this time will be used to good advantage. Most school boards are quite liberal in providing the equipment necessary for these games and play hours.

CHAPTER 6

Secondary Education

TYPES OF SCHOOLS

Secondary education in Canada is considered to be that area of education following upon elementary schooling and preparatory for college and university programmes; it has also been considered as terminal, though this view has been changing with the emergence of the two-year junior or community college. Secondary schools may be academic, vocational, technical, comprehensive, commercial, trade or agricultural. Not many schools may be classified exclusively as one or other of these types for in most instances schools offer a combined programme. The comprehensive or composite school offering a wide variety of programmes is the type proving to be the most popular.

Secondary schools in Canada are of two levels; junior secondary for Grades 7 through 9; and senior secondary for Grades 10 through 13. The junior secondary is designed to provide an exploratory programme for the student who has mastered the fundamental processes in the elementary school by affording him a variety of programmes which will enable him to try his skills in various fields of study and thus facilitate discovery of special interests, talents and skills. As a result of such exploration the student is expected to be able to choose the studies in which he wishes to specialize in the secondary school. Thus, the student who demonstrates an ability to learn languages in the junior secondary grades is advised to specialize in this area in the secondary school and ultimately in the university. Not all school systems in Canada are so organized as to provide this kind of experience, but most large school systems attempt to provide

74

some kind of exploratory experiences. The programme is akin to that of the orientation years in some of the French schools.

CURRICULA

Although there are wide variations in junior secondary school curricula across Canada, for the most part these curricula follow a remarkably similar pattern. Students in the junior secondary school are required to study English, mathematics, social studies, science, physical education, one or more foreign languages and either industrial education or domestic science. Beyond these, and if time and inclination permit the student may also study music, art, commerce, or additional courses in other subject matter areas. As the student proceeds through the school programme he may be permitted to begin specialization by dropping some of the subjects on the programme. Throughout this programme the student is given guidance and counselling with a view to assisting him with making the right decisions in respect of his personal, social, academic and vocational programmes. No decision is recommended by the school without first discussing alternatives with the parents of the student.

Senior secondary school curricula display an even wider variety of forms in Canada. In addition to the academic or university type programme which continues to be the most popular type programme there are commercial, industrial, agricultural and vocational types of programme. In general, students following any one of these programmes will be required to take English, social studies and/or history and geography, physical education and health. In some provinces these required courses or constants will include mathematics and a science, or as in Quebec, some religious studies. The academic or university programme continues to enjoy prestige for it is this programme which provides the student with the widest choices and opportunities, and most parents are anxious that their children at least have the opportunity of beginning the university. Notwithstanding this desire, however, there are still all too many students who are not able to follow this programme for economic as well as intellectual reasons.

HOLDING POWER

The holding power of the senior secondary school varies across Canada, but in the main ranges from approximately 30 per cent in rural areas to about 80 per cent in some urban schools. Between 1911 and 1951 the average years of schooling attained by the Canadian population increased from 8 to 10 years. Since 1951 these figures have advanced with the result that the average years of schooling is approaching 12 years. It is for this reason that more and more industries and commercial houses have been able to require their employees to have a minimum of 12 years of schooling. With the emergence of the two-year junior college as a viable part of more school systems in Canada, it is quite probable that 14 years of schooling will be the norm requirement for entry into the ranks of the employed population.

REVISION

Secondary school programmes in Canada are at present being revised in some instances quite radically. New courses in mathematics, chemistry, physics, literature, and languages are incorporating new developments and findings in each of the fields. Revisions are also taking place in health programmes, music, art, and physical education, as well as in the social sciences. Many of the changes being introduced into the secondary school programmes are based upon studies done in the United States and in England. All too few of the revisions are based upon studies done in Canada. Exceptions to this are the recommendations for change made by the various Royal Commissions on Education appointed by provincial governments. The Report of the Royal Commission of Inquiry on Education in the Province of Quebec Church by the Right Reverend Alphonse Marie Parent released in 1963 through 1966 has been instrumental in bringing about radical changes in the entire Quebec educational system. The Report of the Royal Commission on Education for the Province of British Columbia chaired by Dean S. N. F. Chant brought in recommendations which resulted in 1960 in altering the junior and senior secondary education programmes of the province. In particular, the previous university and general programmes of the secondary school were modified to provide for wider choices by making available six secondary school programmes: academic and technical; commercial; industrial; community services; visual and performing arts; and agriculture. In 1959, two such provincial reports were released: the Report of the Royal Commission on Education in Alberta chaired by the Honourable Senator Donald Cameron; and the Report of the Manitoba Royal Commission on Education chaired by R. O. MacFarlane. Each of these reports with the exception of the last one was instrumental in making significant recommendations for changes in secondary school programmes.

TECHNICAL

Vocational, technical, and technological secondary programmes have been receiving increased attention in Canada in the past decade with special emphasis in the last five years. The Federal Government has subsidized these programmes to a very large extent, by as much as 75 per cent of capital cost for technical schools and technological institutes, and has done so in cooperation with provincial Departments of Education who have been, in most cases, pleased to take advantage of this generosity. The competition for world markets, the increased demand for technical skills in commerce and industry, the decline in the number of skilled people coming to Canada, and the increase in skilled people emigrating to the United States led the Federal Government on the strong recommendations of the Department of Labour and of the Department of Commerce to help finance these programmes. Federal support had a long precedent, however, in the Veteran's Aid programmes which the Federal Government had made available to Second World War veterans and to the educational institutions they attended. These programmes were later to be matched in part by provincial funds as well.

TECHNOLOGICAL

Vocational, technical, technological, and trade school programmes provide for the education of students interested in commercial art; handicrafts such as ceramics, weaving, leather work and jewellery craft; interior design and decoration and furniture design; photographic, radio and television arts; painting, sculpture and engraving. The Ryerson Institute of Technology in Toronto, the British Columbia Technological Institute, the Ecoles des Beaux Arts in Montreal and Quebec, the St. John's Vocational Institute in Newfoundland, and the Southern Alberta Institute of Technology are but a few of the types of institutions to be found in Canada offering technical programmes of one kind or another. Students proceeding to a technological or trade school programme may expect to attend a one-to-four-year programme following completion of the secondary school. In some instances students may pursue studies in vocational programmes preparatory to technical training as part of their regular secondary education studies. An example of the kind of standing students may achieve in these programmes is given by the Alberta College of Art where a student following high school may take a two-year course leading to a general art diploma; a four-year course leading to an advanced diploma in fine art; a four-year course in commercial art leading to an advanced diploma; a three-year diploma course in applied art and general crafts; and a three-year course in pottery and ceramics.

CO-OPERATING ORGANIZATIONS

Both federal and provincial authorities in Canada have been helped by such organizations as the Engineering Institute of Canada, by the Nursing Association, and by the trades unions, who have helped consistently by entering into agreements for apprenticeship programmes with various agencies. Business and industry, however, have failed to give the kind of support to programmes whose beneficiaries would be of help to them. In Europe and in the United States co-operation between education and industry and commerce has advanced to a far greater extent than it has in Canada, and this despite the handsome scholarship programmes which many particular businesses have given to higher education. In 1961–2 the total number of students in publicly and privately sponsored trade, vocational, technical and technological courses was of the order of 206,000 exclusive of those students in engineering courses in universities. The Federal Government's participation in programmes of this kind reaches back to 1919 when the first Technical Education Act was passed on the recommendation of a royal commission which had found that Canada's industries were lagging behind because of a shortage of skilled workers. Relative to programmes in the United States, the U.S.S.R., Japan and Germany, Canada is still lagging, though recent federal expenditure should go far to correcting the imbalance.

GOVERNMENT SCHEDULES

The Special Vocational Training Projects Agreement provides various schedules under which various people may be trained. For example, schedule "M" provides for the training of unemployed persons; schedule "P" for training of persons in primary industries and in home-making; schedule "R" for training of disabled persons; and schedule "K" for the training programmes in the Armed Forces. With the exception of schedule "K", where all costs are borne by the Federal Government, most provinces share the costs of the other schedules. In general these programmes are administered by provincial Departments of Education though other departments such as Health and Industry may be involved in some phases.

EXAMINATIONS

There is a growing trend to have students proceed through the secondary school without formal examinations except for those students who plan to enter the university or other higher educational institution. In lieu of formal end-of-term examinations students are given frequent tests throughout the academic year and are promoted on the basis of these results plus any general assessment which the teachers and counsellors of the students have arrived at over the year. Most schools in Canada have not adopted the European practice of oral examinations, although these were used to some extent in the classical colleges of Quebec. Where end-of-term examinations are written in schools these are given at the end of June. Students who fail on one or more of these papers may write a supplemental paper during the month of August. In recent years there have been developing private tutorial colleges where students who have failed their school examinations may obtain private tuition at a considerable cost to prepare them for a second try at the examinations.

ADMINISTRATION

Secondary schools are generally administered by principals whose primary responsibility is to organize the teaching programme in the school and supervise students and teachers in accordance with the rules and regulations of the local school board and of the Department of Education. In rural situations where there are only one, two, or three rooms in the secondary school, the principal may be expected to teach several subjects in two or more grades as well as administer the school as a whole. In urban areas practices vary quite widely. In schools of five hundred students or less the principal may be called to teach at least one subject; in schools over five hundred his duties are such as to preclude the teaching requirement unless he chooses to teach as some do. Secondary schools in large urban centres such as Montreal, Toronto, and Vancouver may have schools with over

2000 students. In schools of this size the principal may be assisted by one or more vice-principals who share duties with the principal. Where the school has a vocational or technical education department as may occur in a comprehensive school, a vice-principal may supervise this part of the operation. In some instances, as in the Atlantic Provinces, the vice-principal may be expected to administer an evening or adult school programme in addition to his regular duties in the day school.

For the most part, the principals of secondary schools in both urban and rural areas are charged with a multitude of responsibilities many of which are only relatively important to the task of maintaining a good school. Principals must busy themselves with ordering supplies, meeting parents of children who are having difficulties, interviewing salesmen of books and sports equipment, arranging for buses when students and teachers plan a brief tour, entertaining visiting trustees, supervisors and superintendents, and ensuring that the buildings and grounds are being properly taken care of by the caretakers. Since the programme of studies is primarily the responsibility of the Department of Education, the principal has only the responsibility of ensuring that the timetable of the school makes adequate provision for all the required subjects. In this the principal does have the guidelines of the Department but adapting these to the needs of the local school population and the capabilities of his staff is his special task. The principal also has the responsibility of assessing the quality of teaching and this he shares with the specialist supervisor who comes around either from the local superintendency or from the Department of Education. The principal of the secondary school, together with the school's counsellors are also responsible for maintaining liaison with the industrial and commercial community in order that they might be the better able to advise students who elect other than university programmes of study.

GUIDANCE AND COUNSELLING

Most large secondary schools in Canada have counsellors for both boys and girls whose duty it is to advise young people on their social, academic and vocational problems. These counsellors, not always well trained for their jobs, may also be made responsible for administering psychological, intelligence, and aptitude tests in order to ascertain the potentialities of the students for their special interests. In general these counsellors work together with the teachers who work most closely with particular students, and with the parents of these students. Social problems play a very important part in the lives of these adolescent students and their counsellors, many of them former teachers who have been somewhat remote from the hurly-burly of the market place are not always in the best position to enjoy the confidence of the students, with the result that students turn to advisers outside of the school. Again school authorities are becoming aware that personnel in the school able to gain the confidence of students at this age must be mature people who have learned about life in places outside of the pages of a book. The academic problems students face in the secondary schools are many and diverse ranging from a desire to know how to study to making a choice between one course of study and another. In some instances these academic problems derive from the fact that parents have ambitions for their children which are quite unrealistic and it is the job of the counsellor, at times with the co-operation of the principal, to arrange for a change of programme with the consent of the parents and the student. Vocational counselling directs the students' attention to the preparation necessary for particular occupations and the kinds of training expected by employers. Although some counsellors do have work experience which enables them to give sound advice, by far the majority remain too far removed from the world of work to do more than touch upon some of the most obvious aspects. In recent years more counsellors have been obtaining the background training necessary for sound advice to the students.

Canadian schools place a great deal of reliance upon the results of intelligence tests of various sorts, and though the findings of these tests are generally used in conjunction with the results of regular examinations and achievement tests, there is nevertheless a tendency to consider these intelligence scores as essential to any kind of judgement regarding the students' progress. In all too many instances the norms for these intelligence scores are American in origin and can only be used after being modified for the Canadian population. The presence of large numbers of students in the secondary school who are undecided as to the course of study to pursue and who require more evidence than the achievement tests alone can supply necessitates the use of batteries of tests which can serve to guide counsellor, student and parent in making a decision. In a way these intelligence scores help those who are undecided as to a choice of careers to choose on what may be considered an objective basis unrelated to parental or class interests.

INEQUALITIES

There are many inequalities in Canadian secondary education. Many of these inequalities derive from the social and economic disparities which exist between different parts of the country. The student who lives in Montreal or Toronto has a much better chance of attending a school with qualified teachers and good libraries and laboratories than the student who lives in the northern part of either Saskatchewan or Quebec. The dichotomy between rural and urban provisions for education are quite marked across the country, and this inequality takes its toll of many students who on moving to the city find themselves ill prepared either for advanced studies in school or for work.

Despite the fact that the length of the teacher training period has increased over the years, there are still many schools, particularly in remoter parts of the country, who do not have qualified teachers, or teachers inadequately prepared. In consequence there are generations of students in parts of Canada who have not had a well-qualified teacher throughout their elementary school careers.

The cry for equality of educational opportunity has been heard on more than one occasion, but solutions to this problem must wait for a change in the approach to the allocation of teachers and for a change in thinking about remuneration for teachers in remote areas. Several provinces do make special provisions for these isolated areas, but these have proved to be inadequate to attracting teachers for any length of time.

Schools located in wealthy communities quite often have teachers and facilities which are considerably above the average for less-well-endowed areas of a city. In some cases the children of minority groups, as in the case of Indians and Eskimos, but also in the case of new immigrants, do not enjoy the same privileges as do other sectors of the population. Where students come from homes where a second language is spoken equality of opportunity would require that some special teaching of a remedial nature be undertaken, but this is far from being the general practice.

Because there are so few vocational and technical schools in rural areas students here do not have the opportunities of their urban counterparts to attend. One consequence of this inequality in opportunity is that many students in rural areas move to the city without the benefit of the training for which they are best fitted. Even in some cities the specialized type of curricular offerings are not equally available to students in different parts of the city, with the result that some students are penalized unnecessarily at the expense of others.

SCHOOL COUNCILS

In order to provide secondary school students with practical experience in the art of government many schools arrange for the establishment of a school council which, with the advice of members of staff plans student activities and school and community programmes of one kind and another. These councils are elected from the student body and are generally representative of all grades in the school. The responsibilities of these councils vary from school to school, but in the main these councils may arrange

for dances, plays, concerts, teas, game days, and the like programmes and projects. In addition some schools call upon student
councils to arrange for extra-curricular activities such as clubs in
which students can pursue their interests in photography, drama,
literature, science, astronomy, and a variety of hobbies, beyond
the levels dealt with in these areas in the regular curriculum.

Although school councils are supposed to provide students with
experiences designed to prepare them to be good citizens capable
of making responsible decisions in and out of the voting booth,
most school principals reserve the power of veto over all council
decisions. In general student councils appreciate the wisdom of
this type of control and govern themselves and the school accordingly. In a few instances school councils have been given powers
enabling them to exercise disciplinary measures over students
who do not abide by written and unwritten school customs and
regulations. School councils when sitting as courts dealing with
offenders of the school codes are generally very reasonable and
quite fair even though at times their rulings are somewhat more
harsh than a similar finding by school authorities. However, the
ruling of one's peers is always salutary in respect of its ultimate
effects.

REFERENCES

Report of the Manitoba Royal Commission on Education. 1959. Dr. R. O. MacFarlane.
Pp. xxi 284.
Report of the Commission of Inquiry into (British Columbia) Educational Finance. 1945.
Maxwell H. Cameron. Pp. 108.
Report of the Royal Commission of Inquiry on Education in the Province of Quebec. 1963.
Rt. Rev. A. M. Parent. Five volumes.
Report of the Royal Commission on Education in Alberta. 1959. Senator Donald
Cameron. Pp. xxiii 451.
Report of the Royal Commission on Education. British Columbia. 1960. Dr. S. N. F.
Chant. Pp. xviii 460.
H. B. King. *School Finance in British Columbia.* 1935. Commission on School
Finance. Pp. x 230.
D.B.S. *Private Academic, Elementary and Secondary Schools in Canada.* Ottawa:
Queen's Printer, 1959.

CHAPTER 7

Colleges and Universities

HISTORY

Canadian colleges and universities have been influenced in their development by the personnel and traditions of Scottish, French, German, English and American institutions. The result is that present-day higher educational institutions in Canada display a wide variety of traditions very few of which are native to the soil, and many of which are but middling adaptations of the principles which guided the original. Higher education in Canada is generally defined as applying to educational programmes following secondary education, but in practice is taken to refer only to those institutions which are academic in character. In part this stems from the fact that the higher educational institutions in Eastern Canada developed from secondary schools or seminaries, while those in Western Canada coming much later as they did, were originally developed as corporate higher educational institutions.

In 1635 the Colleges des Jesuites laid the basis for higher education in the province of Quebec. This institution became a seminary in 1765 and was incorporated as the University of Laval in 1852. English-language institutions did not appear until the eighteenth century when Canada became British in 1763. In 1790, King's College in Windsor, Nova Scotia, was followed in 1829 by a King's College in Fredericton, New Brunswick, ultimately to become the University of New Brunswick; and in 1827 by a King's College in Toronto, ultimately to become the University of Toronto. These early institutions were originally all denominational in character, and privately supported. When public monies became available to these institutions the denominational character was in several instances played down in their programmes. McGill University in Montreal was incorporated in 1821 as a non-denominational institution and set a precedent for the period. Confederation in 1867 led to the establishment of several provinces in Western Canada, and these in turn established non-denominational institutions: Manitoba in 1877; British Columbia in 1890; Alberta in 1906; and Saskatchewan in 1907. In addition to these provincially supported universities there were in addition denominational colleges established in Western Canada in these years: United College in Winnipeg; Brandon College in Brandon; Campion College in Regina; and Union College in Vancouver. Although non-denominational colleges and universities have developed, most institutions are still independent or religiously affiliated. Nonetheless, all institutions are in receipt of federal funds designed to subsidize though not fully support higher education.

DISTRIBUTION

There are in Canada approximately 350 higher educational institutions distributed as follows: Newfoundland, 3; Prince Edward Island, 2; Nova Scotia, 16; New Brunswick, 9; Quebec, 212; Ontario, 65; Manitoba, 10; Saskatchewan, 17; Alberta, 11; and British Columbia, 10. In the 1963–4 academic year there were enrolled in these institutions 160,000 students of which number about 10,000 were working on a second or third degree. Of the total enrolment shown approximately 8500 students were from the United States, Commonwealth countries, West Indies, Africa, China, South-east Asia, Philippines and elsewhere. By far the largest portion of students were enrolled in arts, science and commerce programmes, with the next largest group in teacher training, library science and social service. The applied sciences, medicine and related fields, law and theology, art, music and journalism also attracted sizeable bodies of students.

ORGANIZATION AND ADMINISTRATION

Each university and college in Canada is headed by a board of governors. The members of the board may be elected or appointed. Where universities are supported by provincial funds, the provincial government will reserve the right to appoint one or more members to the board. Board meetings are chaired by the Chancellor who follows the agenda submitted by the Vice-Chancellor or President of the university. The President of the university is responsible for administering the institution in line with the policies established by the board. Responsibility for academic policy is vested in the Senate, a body made up of representatives elected by alumni of the university, by various lay and professional organizations in the community, and by the staff of the university. The board of governors is guided in its overall policy decisions by what Senate has to say about academic affairs. As a result of a study of university government in 1965, it is probable that in the near future, professors of the university will be represented on the board of governors, and students will be represented on Senate. Both moves have been long overdue. In a sense these two moves suggest that those most closely affected by university policies should have a say in their formulation.

Canadian university students generally begin their studies in September and continue through two semesters until the end of April or May. In the main, the major term break is at Christmas with only one or two days off at Easter. Most of the universities provide for a brief third term of six or seven weeks during July and August. This term is generally referred to as the summer school session. Some of the newer universities are experimenting with a three-semester system. Many universities offer courses for credit at evening sessions, and where there are extension or adult education departments, credit and non-credit courses at rural centres in the province. These courses will usually run the regular term.

Universities are organized into faculties, schools or colleges, each unit being administered by a dean or head. Each faculty may be subdivided into departments with a separate chairman. These faculties are autonomous with respect to academic affairs, but come under the general regulations of the university in all other matters. Students on entry to the university register with a particular faculty, but may take courses in more than one faculty. The separate faculties have their programmes interlocked by way of committees and calendars, and through the overall supervision of the Senate as represented in each of the aforesaid faculties.

FINANCE

Canadian universities receive approximately half of their revenue from government sources, mainly provincial, and about half their revenue from a combination of student fees, endowments, miscellaneous grants, and occasional sources such as public subscriptions. In 1961, for example, Canada's total university expenditure of $176 million was made up of $5 million from endowments; $110 million from government grants; $46 million from student fees; and miscellaneous sources accounted for approximately $15 million. Canadian universities have suffered from a shortage of funds, particularly since the period following the Second World War demonstrated that many more young people were planning to seek a university education. Furthermore, it had become increasingly evident that there were in Canada grave disparities between one part of the country and another in the matter of equality of educational opportunity for higher education, particularly as the resources of the different provinces varied so greatly. The increase in demand for higher education was not met by an increase in facilities or by an increase in the monies made available to those who were economically deprived. In 1965 the Federal Government did make available a series of interest free loans for needy students, but this only touches the real problem, those who had the ability but needed their entire cost defrayed until such time as they were in a position to earn money.

COURSES AND PROGRAMMES

Most universities in Canada are organized around faculties, schools or colleges each devoted to a particular field. Most universities provide courses of study in arts, science, social science, and the humanities for both graduate and undergraduate students. The larger institutions will also have schools of law, medicine, engineering and architecture, commerce, education, home economics, agriculture and social work. In most instances these professional schools are interlocked with arts and science programmes where students obtain their basic course work before entering upon professional studies.

The student who seeks admission to a university must submit a certificate showing he has completed the eleventh, twelfth or thirteenth grade of an academic high school programme. In a few instances students are required to write examinations or a series of tests to qualify for entrance to the university. More colleges and universities now provide guidance and counselling services for their students, and frequently the personnel of these departments consult with school counsellors before making a final recommendation regarding the placing of the student on any particular programme.

Although requirements vary from one institution to another, the Bachelor's degree is awarded after three or four years of study; the Master's degree after one or two additional years; and the Doctor's degree after the completion of an acceptable research study and report. The requirements for professional degrees also vary widely but in the main students have to spend from three to five years in a programme. French language institutions in Quebec have different requirements. The student in Quebec who wishes a B.A. humanities degree enters an eight-year course of study in a college classique from Grade 7 in an elementary school; if, however, the Quebec student wishes a science degree, he stays in the secondary school programme through Grade 11 following which he enters the university. More recently, and following the reform of 1960, students in Quebec wishing either a science or humanities degree may enter a university. If the recommendations of the Parent Commission on education are adopted then the French pattern of education centring in the classical colleges will be altered entirely in favour of a system more nearly akin to the English language pattern.

French and English universities in Canada play an important part in the cultural life of the communities in which they are located. Adult education programmes, evening courses, and special refresher courses are also provided for those sectors of the population who wish to take advantage of these offerings. In addition, each university provides some type of correspondence programme for those students who for one reason or another are unable to attend regular sessions; only partial credit towards a degree may be obtained in this way. Summer sessions attract large numbers of students, particularly teachers, who wish to upgrade their professional credentials, or embark upon new types of courses entirely. In some institutions, the academic year is divided into three semesters obviating the need for a summer session, the third semester serving in lieu of it.

RESEARCH

In addition to providing instruction at the university and affording various educational services to the community at large, each university engages in research of one kind and another. The members of each department are expected to make contribution to knowledge as a part of their regular work, and many do so. However, much more could be done in Canada, not so much because there is a disinterest on the part of individuals as because university and college administrations have had difficulty in convincing provincial government officials that such expenditures are fully justified in terms of long-term results. The Social Science Research Council, the National Science Research Council, and the Canada Council have been instrumental in supporting and stimulating research, but the funds available from these national sources are limited. Many Canadian personnel and universities have been fortunate in enjoying the generosity of American foundations and scholarships, but these have only served to highlight the limited vision of Canadian sources and contributors.

Scientific and technical research have been encouraged and stimulated by developments associated with the World Wars. In each case industrial, technical and scientific advances were made to meet the needs identified in and out of universities in the pursuit of solutions to social, economic and political problems. Although many of these programmes were associated with universities there were programmes in industry and commerce. The railways, the hydro-electric corporations, the pulp and paper industry, the agricultural organizations, the oil industry and the fishing and mining industries have all maintained separate research laboratories and these have been linked in many ways to research programmes in higher educational institutions. Both provincial and federal authorities have come to recognize that the State must contribute much more than it has in the past to the stimulation and funding of research of all types.

Health and physical educational programmes have enjoyed good support from provincial and federal Departments of Health and Welfare, and these bodies have provided large sums of money for research in medicine and in health. However, here as elsewhere much more could be done. The adoption of medicare programmes and a general national health scheme will probably release funds for more research. In recent years provincial governments have either alone or in concert with others established research councils to assist in finding solutions to industrial, commercial, and transportation problems: and to make available research resources to small industry that ordinarily could not provide these for themselves. The British Columbia Research Council, the Nova Scotia Research Foundation, the Research Council of Alberta, and the Ontario Research Foundation are representative of the organizations engaged in these research programmes. Despite these agencies, however, it is worth noting that more than half of all expenditures in research have taken place in industries associated with transportation, electricity and chemistry. The Federal Government expenditures on all forms of re-research amounted to about $335 million in 1965; industrial research amounted to about $120 million. Expenditures by provincial governments and research agencies on research at the local level need to be added to the aforementioned figures.

STUDENTS

Canadian university and college enrolment reached a total of approximately 180,000 students in 1965. Higher education programmes of other types, e.g. correspondence classes, classical colleges, amounted in total to an additional 125,000 students. Women students represented 30 per cent of full-time university enrolment, 40 per cent of part-time programmes, and 54 per cent of correspondence courses. There were in 1965 about 32,000 bachelors degrees granted; about 4000 masters degrees, and about 500 doctoral degrees. The range and variety of studies engaged in by these students is represented in part by these fields: agriculture, architecture, arts and science, commerce, chiropractic, dentistry, education, engineering, fine and applied arts, forestry, home economics, journalism, law, medicine, music, nursing, optometry, pharmacy, social work, theology, and veterinary science. From the aforementioned data it may be inferred that Canadian colleges and universities provide for a broad spectrum of professional studies which European universities normally leave to allied and associated institutions. Nevertheless, basic studies are not neglected in Canada for of a total of approximately 45,000 students who received degrees in 1965, 15,000 were awarded for studies in arts and science, and 15,000 in professional programmes.

In keeping with practices elsewhere Canadian colleges and universities provide for the education of overseas students in considerable numbers. The total enrolment in all kinds of institutions in 1964 approached 9000. These students came from Africa, Asia, Europe, Central America and Mexico, Oceania and the West Indies. With the exception of students from the United States, the students from Asia, Europe and the West Indies constituted the largest overseas contingents in universities. In all students came to Canada from 150 different countries, though the largest group-ings came from Commonwealth areas.

Although many students and their families are financially able to afford the costs of attending institutions of higher education, there are still large numbers of students unable to do so. In 1964 the Federal Government increased its per student grant to the universities and made available an extended series of scholarships for both undergraduate and graduate students. Nevertheless it is estimated that about 25 to 40 per cent of students who graduate from the high schools and have demonstrated capacity for uni-versity work are unable for economic reasons to attend. On the other hand, the 40 to 60 per cent failure rate among first year university students suggests that there are many who ought not to attend. The Canadian university differs from its European coun-terpart with respect to the selective procedures adopted. The costs of higher education are such that many students engage in part-time work, particularly during the summers when the Canadian economy can afford to absorb this additional labour force. Boys have a better chance of obtaining types of work from which the remuneration is sufficient to finance a full academic year. Girls are more likely to be supported by their families. Another phenomenon which has been showing a marked increase among university students is the married couple. In most instances the wife will work to help finance her husband's education, and where circumstances are such that both are able to attend, will maintain a home, including children, on or near campuses where it has become increasingly the practice to provide special housing for young marrieds.

CHAPTER 8

Teachers and Technologies

CURRENT

Teachers for elementary and secondary schools are trained either in normal schools or teacher training colleges and in faculties of education. There are 125 teacher training colleges in Canada for some 20,000 students and 25 faculties of education providing for another 12,000 students. The teacher training colleges provide, in the main, a two-year programme following secondary school graduation for those who wish to teach primary and elementary schools, while the faculties of education, located on university campuses, provide a variety of programmes lasting anywhere from two to five years and enabling the graduate to teach either in elementary or secondary schools.

HISTORY

The first normal school in Canada was opened in Quebec in 1836 and took its pattern and tradition from the French and German models which dated from the seventeenth century. Despite this tradition the influence of Horace Mann of the United States was also felt in shaping the pattern of teacher training in Canada. The monitorial schools made provision for the training of teachers and in doing so anticipated the need for preparing for education of the masses. Normal schools spread rapidly throughout the country and by the first quarter of the twentieth century standards for entry had been raised to Grade 12 or 13. By this time too, secondary teachers were being prepared in university faculties and summer session programmes for teachers had been established. In the period following the Second World War teacher training colleges joined faculties of education of university campuses for the training of elementary as well as secondary teachers. The provinces of Newfoundland, Manitoba, Saskatchewan, Alberta and British Columbia provide for all teacher education on university campuses. In Ontario, Quebec, and the Atlantic Provinces for both geographical and historical reasons normal schools and faculties of education remain separate.

ELEMENTARY TEACHERS

To gain admittance to a teacher training college students are required to complete a secondary school academic programme. In the course of two years of training the student spends approximately two-thirds of his time on professional training and about a third reviewing academic material. This two-year programme also requires the student to engage in practice teaching for some six weeks in each year. More and more elementary teachers have been going on to further study with the result that an increasing proportion of the elementary school teaching population has at least one university degree. Too large a percentage of the elementary teachers in Canada teach for only about three years following entry to the profession after which they marry or go to other fields of work. Men who go into elementary teaching are relatively few in number in the beginning, and of these few many aim to become elementary school principals or go on to teaching in the secondary schools. The largest number of these teachers, men and women alike, come from the lower and middle economic levels and bring to the school the value systems of this area of society. In Quebec, and in French communities across Canada, many elementary teachers are recruited from lay and religious orders; in some cases brothers of the religious orders teach at this level as well.

Nursery and kindergarten teachers are prepared in normal schools and faculties of education as well, but in most instances, the training for this category of worker is not as well defined as it is for other levels. For the most part where there are public nurseries and kindergartens these are in charge of qualified personnel; private institutions are generally not so fortunate. In one city at least provision has been made to have children begin formal schooling at four years of age, but in general nursery and kindergarten programmes begin at five years.

SECONDARY TEACHERS

Although secondary teachers were originally recruited to schools from universities and grammar school graduates, by the time of the First World War these were being prepared in faculties of education located on campuses of universities. In general students entered a faculty for one year of professional training following achievement of an arts or science degree, but in some instances students could take a briefer course to qualify for certification. The one-year post arts or science professional training year is still prevalent. A second type of programme has been developed, originally at Alberta, then in Newfoundland, British Columbia and Saskatchewan, in which the student can pursue a combined academic and professional programme of studies leading to a Bachelor of Education degree and to certification to teach in a secondary school. This new type of programme which has been in vogue now for some fifteen years is still experimental, and in some instances students have found it unsatisfactory as a preparatory experience, especially in so far as it has required the student to swing between two or more goals throughout his study years. One of the main problems confronting the integrated programme is that of balancing academic and professional work for the student and arranging for correlation of effort on the part of arts and education faculties. Ontario, British Columbia and Nova Scotia are the three provinces in Canada with the largest proportion of secondary teachers with university degrees.

Except for the period of the depression when employment opportunities in many areas of business and industry were limited and many turned to teaching, Canada has never had an adequate supply of teachers for its secondary schools and particularly for its vocational and technical programmes. Many provincial Departments of Education, especially those in Western Canada, adopted the practice of sending recruiting teams to England, Scotland, Ireland and Wales to invite teachers to take service in Canada. In recent years, particularly because of the relatively better salaries to be found in Canada, several thousand have been taking advantage of these offers. However, it is a serious question whether this practice is entirely ethical since Britain has its own teacher shortages and can ill afford the luxury of training people for a country that can better afford to do so. One of the anomalies contributing to this situation is the fact that all teacher training costs in Britain are borne by the Government while in Canada prospective teachers are required to pay their own tuition and living costs while training. Some bursaries and scholarships are available to a few of the best students but these are all too few and do not by any means take care of even the best students.

VOCATIONAL TEACHERS

Although vocational education has been a part of the educational pattern of offerings since the First World War, the preparation of teachers for this area of the curriculum has been a matter of chance. Many of the teachers of vocational classes were recruited from the ranks of skilled craftsmen in industry, and after a brief in-service type of preparation were certified for teaching. More recently teachers of vocational and technical classes have been prepared in special industrial arts programmes of schools of education, though the earlier pattern of preparation has not entirely disappeared. The growth and development of secondary industry in Canada following the Second World War pointed up the scarcity of people skilled in many trades essential to the economy of the country with the result that the Federal Government became concerned to the extent of taking definite action. The Vocational Training Coordination Act of 1942 was replaced in 1960 by the Technical and Vocational Training Assistance Act which stimulated marked development of programmes across Canada. Among other things this Act provided for the Federal Government's defraying 75 per cent of capital expenditures for building and equipping vocational training facilities. The following table indicates the extent to which the provincial governments took advantage of this support:

CAPITAL PROJECTS APPROVED UNDER THE TECHNICAL AND VOCATIONAL TRAINING AGREEMENT, APRIL 1961 TO MARCH 31, 1963.

Province or Territory	Projects	Total cost	Federal share	New student places
Newfoundland	15	28,258,258	21,055,075	3670
Prince Edward Island	6	2,754,072	2,065,555	1380
Nova Scotia	14	9,589,506	7,191,629	2704
New Brunswick	14	7,374,381	4,792,504	2215
Quebec	87	44,598,051	23,743,419	7603
Ontario	259	319,915,532	200,089,747	98,556
Manitoba	56	7,037,562	4,934,802	2180
Saskatchewan	8	16,957,584	8,224,611	3654
Alberta	33	49,924,849	36,994,715	11,575
British Columbia	19	19,771,312	13,585,168	4328
Yukon Territory	1	909,062	682,796	144
Northwest Territories	1	480,000	64,800	30
Canada	513	507,570,169	323,424,821	138,039

Canada Year Book, 1963–64, p. 739.

In consequence of the foregoing provisions it is evident that opportunities for learning trade skills of various kinds will not be lacking, and that teachers for these programmes will ultimately be forthcoming. The Technical and Vocational Training Agreement provides for: (1) a technical and vocational high school programme; (2) technician training; (3) trade and other occupational training; (4) training in co-operation with industry; (5) training of the unemployed; (6) training of the disabled; (7) training of technical and vocational teachers; (8) training for federal

departments and agencies; (9) student aid; and (10) apprenticeship training. This scheme, comprehensive and geared to the
economic and professional needs of the country, is designed to
keep Canada abreast of modern technological developments.

TECHNICAL AND TECHNOLOGICAL FACILITIES

The rapid growth in industrial and commercial technologies
has necessitated the development of a class of schools which
provide training in technologies at levels beyond those obtaining
in secondary institutions. Schools of the order of the Alberta
Institute of Technology in Edmonton, the Nova Scotia Institute
of Technology in Halifax, the British Columbia Institute of
Technology in Burnaby, the Ryerson Institute in Toronto, offer
programmes in broadcast communications; building technology;
chemical and metallurgical technology; civil and structural services; hotel, motel and restaurant management; medical laboratory and radio graphytechnology; mining and surveying; and in
several other areas. The technological revolution has revolution-
ized the level of training required for service in many occupations
and the increase in attendance at these institutions attests the
recognition accorded them.

Of the approximately 200 vocational and technical schools to
be found in Canada, about 25 offer post-secondary training in
various technologies. These post-secondary programmes, however, though emphasizing the acquisition of particular sets of
skills, nevertheless require the student to achieve a measure of
general education consistent with the level of his technical training. Thus, throughout these technological programmes there runs
a thread of general education in the form of courses in writing and
contemporary thought, human relations, economics, English,
mathematics, modern literature, and the like. It is evident from
this constellation of offerings that the demands of a technological
society may be met without entirely sacrificing the values of a
general education for those who are technically minded.

UNIVERSITIES

The universities in Canada play their part in contributing to meeting the technical and technological needs of the country. Schools and faculties of engineering, applied science, architecture, agriculture, forestry, and commerce are engaged in providing for the refinement of the theoretical basis upon which to shape practical programmes in each of the aforementioned areas. Research projects in these fields are supported by federal funds and by funds supplied by business and industry. The oil and chemical companies of Canada maintain respectable laboratories in which a good deal of research goes on, and organizations such as the British Columbia Research Council, of which there are several in Canada, provide research facilities for companies not large enough to support their own. Universities also have computer centres which provide services not only to their own faculties but to commercial, industrial and engineering organizations who wish to take advantage of these.

ADULT EDUCATION

The rate at which technological developments have taken place in all sectors of society has made it incumbent upon many people, professional and skilled alike, to upgrade their educations. In Canada, as elsewhere, it has been estimated that no trade or professional person can remain outside of a classroom or lecture for longer than four or five years. Adult education has grown apace over the years with the result that enrolled in a wide variety of programmes are approximately a million people. These adult education programmes, many of which are designed to upgrade the technical and technological backgrounds of workers and students alike cover a wide range of offerings. Adult education programmes cover the study of foreign languages, money management, literature, mathematics, landscaping, sign painting, aviation ground school, typewriting, economics, public speaking, speed reading, drafting, automobile mechanics, theatre, dress-making, sailing, wood carving, and a host of other types of study. In some instances medical schools will conduct refresher courses for general and specialist practitioners, and engineering institutes will do likewise for their engineers. According to a D.B.S. survey in 1960:

> "About 40 per cent of evening students were enrolled in vocational courses and classes offered by school boards, with assistance from the provincial departments, or by universities and colleges. About as many were enrolled in non-credit courses of general cultural value, and the remainder attended classes leading to a high school diploma or university degree. Some 25 government departments supported such classes, which enrolled almost 8,000 in elementary and about 70,000 in secondary school subjects; 212,000 were enrolled in vocational courses of whom almost 100,000 were taking home economics or agriculture; and in the general classes 84,000 were enrolled in social education, 28,500 in the fine arts and 20,000 in other related courses."*

In addition there are lectures, exhibits, tours, music and art programmes offered by a wide variety of agencies for short or long periods which attract something of the order of half a million people. Radio and television educational programmes account for another large sector of the adult population who are interested in furthering their general and special interests.

APPRENTICESHIP

Despite the wide variety of educational and trade training opportunities available there are still a number of occupations which depend upon an apprenticeship programme for the training of craftsmen. Trades for which apprenticeship training is required include aeronautical mechanics, auto-body and fender repair, boiler shop worker, boat builder, bricklayer and stonemason, carpenter, draughtsman, electrical maintenance, jewellery and watch repair, millwright, plasterer, refrigeration worker, shipwright, stationary engineer, steel fabrication worker, and a host of others. Not all provinces require apprenticeship training, differences in requirements depending to a large extent upon the

---

* Dominion Bureau of Statistics, *A Graphic Presentation of Canadian Education*, 1961, p. 42.

arrangements made with the union and labour organizations involved in a particular trade. The Canadian Labour Congress, the Confederation of National Trade Unions, and various other independent organizations among them take a keen interest in vocational, technical and technological programmes and assist in the establishment of guidelines for apprenticeship requirements. The effects of automation and of similar technologies has alerted many of the unions to the need for broadly-based support for re-education programmes of all kinds.

IMMIGRATION

The Canadian economy still depends to a very large extent upon the trade and professional skills which come to its shores each year with immigrants from many lands. Though there is a steady drain of these skills to the United States approaching some 500 people a month, this drain has been partially compensated for by new arrivals. Although Canada's educational institutions have been increasing their collective capacity to prepare people for an increasingly technological society they have not been able to graduate enough to meet the demand. Canadian immigration policy has been tailored to select skilled people from abroad in order to ensure enough people to man the needs of an expanding economy. Canadian schools, colleges and universities continue to bring in teachers, particularly from the British Isles where salaries and teaching conditions are not as satisfactory as they are in some parts of Canada.

CLOSED CIRCUIT TELEVISION AND RADIO BROADCASTING

Educational, industrial and commercial organizations are turning to closed circuit television to facilitate the dissemination of information and make it possible for the largest number of people possible to benefit from instruction and demonstration of recent developments. Closed circuit television is being used successfully in the entire range of schools from elementary through the university. Schools of medicine have done an excellent job of televising operations and schools of dentistry have done likewise. Steel mills and paper and lumber enterprises also make effective use of television. The effective use of television has been extended by the development of video tapes, and by the use of direct cable and microwave connections. Although these television outlets were originally to be found mainly in urban centres, these now extend to school systems in town and country. To an increasing extent the Canadian Broadcasting Corporation and independent television stations have been providing educational TV for schools and colleges as well as for the general public. In 1963 there were in Canada 14 C.B.C. television stations as well as 95 rebroadcasting and network relay stations; and in addition 134 privately owned television and relay stations. This network of television stations makes it possible to reach about 92 per cent of the population.

Canada's radio stations reach about 98 per cent of the population including those people who live beyond the Arctic Circle on the shores and islands of the Arctic Ocean. Each Department of Education has had an audio-visual branch for many years and these in co-operation with the Canadian Broadcasting Corporation plan many school programmes. The fields of drama, of literature, of science, of art, and of physical education receive attention in depth. With the advent of reasonably priced tapes it is now possible for many of the broadcasts to be fitted into regular school programmes rather easily.

PROGRAMMED LEARNING AND COMPUTERS

The use of computers and programmed learning devices has been increasing in both public and private educational agencies. Though the computer-teacher has not appeared in Canada as he has in the United States, computers are being made use of in connection with research in business and industry, with the teaching of mathematics, with the organization of the time-table, with research in linguistics, and with library listings and recordings. Teaching machines and a variety of devices for developing programmed learning have been increasing in numbers and have become more sophisticated as teaching tools. More school systems have been experimenting with these teaching aids and more teachers have begun to accommodate the idea that these are useful assistants.

CHAPTER 9

Forms and Reforms

BUILDINGS AND GROUNDS

The physical facilities provided for Canada's educational enterprise are today among the best to be found in the world. Not all provincial governments are equally liberal, but all, for the most part, attempt to provide the best facilities they can afford. Modern engineering and architecture have combined with other disciplines such as medicine and psychology to produce educational buildings which conduce to creating good learning situations. The little red school house of yesteryear, the one-room affair to be found in most school districts a generation ago, has all but disappeared. These one-room schools are still to be found in remote rural areas, generally in the northernmost parts of the provinces, but elsewhere they have been replaced, even in small towns and villages, by consolidated schools made up of two or more classrooms at least. These larger establishments make it possible for schools to have an auditorium, a cafeteria, a gymnasium, an all purpose room, such specialized classes as art rooms, music rooms, and in some cases, even swimming pools. Only the very largest schools can justify having all of the aforementioned facilities, and only the very wealthiest provinces can afford to provide these, but despite these factors there are many schools with several of the special facilities described.

Changes in the psychology of classroom learning have led to changes in school design. Elementary and secondary schools now have classrooms of different sizes to permit of variation in programmes. The traditional concept of one-class-one-teacher has given way to team teaching arrangements whereby several

106

teachers co-operate in instruction in one or more classes. As a result of these changes there have been further changes in the architecture of schools such that in some instances instructional space is no longer entirely confined within four walls but is open on one or two sides. Along with these developments in team teaching have been further developments in programmed learning calling for the individualization of instructional space. The large group meeting has been balanced by the smaller than average group, in many instances the individual alone. Again, school libraries, though still sadly deficient in many systems do provide individual study spaces which not too long ago were thought to be a pretentious frill unnecessary below the college level.

The changes wrought in the classroom building have been matched to a very considerable extent by changes in school grounds. These grounds are now, in many instances, conceived of as play and exercise fields, and as extensions of classroom learning situations. Too, these grounds are designed to serve the average student who is only interested in maintaining good health and not in achieving fame either as an athlete or as a callisthenic expert. More attention is being paid as well to group games with the result that most students in school are involved in one or more physical activities for longer periods. Although most schools are coeducational and several athletic programmes are conducted on this basis, most physical education programmes are so arranged as to separate the sexes. As might be expected schools in rural areas usually have the largest school grounds, but there are exceptionally few schools in Canada in urban areas that do not have some sizeable setting for playgrounds.

ADMINISTRATIVE CLIMATES

The image of the stern schoolmaster riding herd on a class of fidgeting children unwilling to learn sums and abide by school disciplines has practically disappeared in Canada. Today's teachers are on average better educated and more often people who have chosen teaching as a profession. Not too long ago, too many classrooms in Canada were staffed by people who had drifted into teaching as an escape from more challenging adult occupations, and behaved accordingly. These same drifters imposed disciplines which were excessively harsh and quite often unreasonable. By contrast today's child-oriented teacher is better able to engage the child in study and educational activities.

Nevertheless, the authoritarian character of school administration still obtains in many quarters. With all responsibility for education vested in provincial legislatures and the authority for exercising this responsibility vested in ministers of education who have no countervailing authority in Ottawa, there is a tendency for administrative climates in schools and colleges to reflect this authoritarian hierarchy. Teachers, principals, supervisors, directors and superintendents are made constantly aware of the views of provincial Departments of Education whose personnel have generally come up through the same system. One consequence of this excessive inbreeding is an excessive emphasis upon provincialism which comes to permeate the entire educational climate. Another and more serious consequence of this state of affairs is the tendency to conservatism and conformity. Where custom and tradition are exercised through family compacts the place for innovation is relegated to the bottom of the table. It is unfortunate in the extreme that the administrative climates to be found in many Canadian school systems are diametrically opposed to the democratic principles which are supposed to be the guidelines for all Canadian institutions.

ROYAL COMMISSIONS

Every society has its characteristic mode of bringing about needed reforms in its social institutions. In Canada the educational enterprise is modified periodically on the basis of recommendations made by royal commissions appointed by provincial governments when these feel that their educational systems are no longer in tune with the times. Between 1959 and 1963 four major Royal

Commission Reports on Education were prepared, all of them influential in bringing about needed reforms. The Chant Commission Report on Education in British Columbia, the MacFarlane Report of Manitoba, the Cameron Report of Alberta, and the Parent Report of Quebec were all instrumental in recommending changes in the pattern of elementary, secondary, technical and teacher training programmes. Though the reports differ from one another in respect of the differences in their particular educational institutions and social conditions, all of them have recommended more education for more people for longer periods of time; suggested the expenditures of larger sums of money on every level of education; provided for more choices in secondary school programmes; more facilities for further education by way of community college and technical education institutions; more aggressive in-service policies for the up-dating of teachers of science, languages and mathematics; special attention to exceptional and underprivileged children.

The most far-reaching and radical reforms are those of the Parent Commission for Quebec. This Commission produced a report in five volumes which deals with the entire structure and function of the educational systems of Quebec. This Commission began its studies by tracing the entire history of the development of education in Quebec from 1608 through five clearly defined periods to 1960 when the Commission began its work. One significant change suggested, the abolishment of the duality, Protestant and Catholic systems, and the appointment of a single Minister of Education. Other organizational recommendations are as radical, and if adopted, should go far to bringing more efficient administration to the system. In particular provision is made for a drastic reduction in the influence of the Church on educational policies and programmes. This commission was particularly concerned with modernizing an educational system which had lost touch with reality and was rapidly losing the confidence of the youth of Quebec. As the report states in one section: "Canada and Quebec have shared very little in the world's scientific, literary, artistic, philosophical and theological life," and goes on to suggest that a new look in education is required. This new long look encompasses views that seek a more social and a less competitive school, a school which recognizes cultural pluralism as a viable component of its educational philosophy, a school which inculcates respect for intelligence, appreciation of moral values, and which looks to graduating students who are versed in science and technology as they are in the humanities and the classics.

The Cameron Report of Alberta and the Chant Report for British Columbia both emphasized the need for schools to recognize that their special responsibility was to the intellectual development of the child. Both reports recommended courses and programmes which would serve the needs of rapidly changing societies. Since these reports were prepared for societies in transition from primary to secondary producers it was deemed essential in both instances to stress the need for courses of study which would prepare individuals for newly developing industries. The Parent Report also recommended the schools give special attention to mathematics, science and technical education. In addition this Commission suggested that more attention be given to languages, music, the plastic arts and films in schools. The Parent Report went even further and suggested that serious attention be given to moral education as distinct from religious studies. It is rather significant that no one of the other reports has given the same emphasis to this basic criterion for human development.

However wise the recommendations of royal commissions for educational reform, changes actually brought about are dependent upon the willingness of elected and appointed government officials to implement any recommendations. The Chant Commission report in British Columbia is an example of a report whose major recommendations were implemented despite the carping arguments of critics. On the other hand the Hope Report on Education died aborning because the government of the day feared the wrath of school officials and voters alike.

JUNIOR COLLEGES

Among the significant changes which have been taking place in Canada has been the emergence of the junior, community, or district college as it is variously known in different parts of Canada. Originally developed in the United States where there are a thousand such institutions now, the Canadian junior college was first established in Alberta from where it has spread to British Columbia, Ontario and Quebec. In Quebec the junior college will probably succeed to the place formerly occupied by the classical college, but elsewhere it will occupy the same place it does in American educational systems, between the secondary school and the university. Ever since the Second World War it has become evident that the transition from the secondary school to the university was too abrupt for many students and that an intermediate stage was desirable. American experience demonstrated that a wide variety of programmes at a stage intermediate between the secondary school and the university enabled many students to make choices they had been unable to do otherwise.

Junior college programmes range from the strictly academic type to be found in the first and second year of the university to technical specialties such as nursing and X-ray technicians to technological programmes of the order of computer operation and the like areas. In general junior colleges provide for two-year programmes in all areas leading to third year university and technological institute courses. Those students for whom two years is sufficient to qualify for a specialty may graduate on a terminal programme without prejudice to any later interest they may have in further study. In some schools, junior college students may change from one programme to another during the first year in an attempt to settle upon a satisfying field, but must by the beginning of the second year have made a definite choice. Most students are able to do so. The value of the junior college is that it permits late developers to opt for further study; those affected by automation or technology to obtain retraining in a brief period; those students who having left school wish to return to an educational climate more in keeping with their maturity than that to be found in a secondary school. One of the most interesting results of the junior college programme is the increase in the number of students who seek to go to the university from its halls.

EXCEPTIONAL CHILDREN

The education of exceptional children has been receiving increased attention in the past two decades. The increase in the number of major work classes for gifted students identified early in the elementary school, and far enriched courses of study for students in the secondary school has been marked. Most public school systems in Canada today make some provision for the gifted and the talented student and though much more remains to be done in this realm, there is recognition that special talents require special facilities and special personnel. Most schools, too, attempt to establish advanced classes for students who demonstrate more than ordinary capability in science, in art, or in writing. In some instances school boards make special provisions for these students by allowing additional teachers in a school in order to reduce overall class size.

Special classes and schools are also provided for the deaf, dumb and blind, for the mentally retarded, and for the physically and emotionally disabled. In some cities there are child guidance clinics organized to provide special psychological, psychometric, psychiatric, social work and tutorial services for all children who require special attention. Provincial Departments of Education are giving increasing attention to this area of education and though they have been slow to do so, parents and teachers have been leading the battle for recognition with a good measure of success. The medical profession has been very active in this area of education, and have been successful in helping establish special clinics for children who were spastic, tubercular or suffering from one ailment or another. For the most part these special facilities are available in larger centres only, but more recently travelling clinics are beginning to make their appearance so that children of remote areas may receive special attention as well.

The Federal Department of Health and Welfare has been supportive of those special education programmes by providing funds for special facilities and by affording special financial assistance to people interested in specializing in the education of abnormal and exceptional children. Teachers and supervisors of these special education programmes still have to go to the United States or to England or France for advanced training, but Canadian programmes are beginning to appear as in the case of speech and hearing in Manitoba and special education in British Columbia. With the increase in the number of hospitals specializing in children's ailments, and an increase in federal and provincial funds for supporting extra services there has been a general improvement in attitude toward the disabled child. An interesting side effect of the additional attention being given these programmes is the change in attitude on the part of employers who have begun to appreciate the fact that a disabled body may hold a fully developed human being.

CURRICULAR CHANGES

The traditional patterns of elementary and secondary education have been undergoing radical changes in both content and method. The old elementary pattern of reading, writing and arithmetic has been altered to include social studies, art and music and kindred fields. As well, the student has been freed from memorizing long lists of facts in favour of providing him with the skills which enable him to acquire these when he needs them. The traditional reliance upon one text and one teacher has been changed to allow for the recognition of more than one authority whether of person or text. The absolute and authoritarian character of learning and study has given way in the field of curriculum to recognition of the role of relative values. The student who was formerly counselled to accept all that the school offered on faith and without challenge is now confronted with an intellectual renaissance which is proving both challenging and exciting.

Some of the most radical changes have taken place in science and mathematics. In the fields of chemistry, physics and biology many laboratories have been provided to enable the student to discover for himself the principles upon which these sciences have developed. In the fields of arithmetic and mathematics changes have been introduced in the elementary school as well as in the secondary and though some of these changes have been controversial several of the modifications have proved to be worthwhile. In all too many cases, however, these changes in science and mathematics have been based upon research and study conducted in the United States. The American studies in biology, in physics and in chemistry and the textbooks and programmes which were published in connection with them have been applied almost completely in Canada. Such modifications as have been introduced have been limited to relatively minor points to accommodate local phenomena. Changes have also been introduced in the course of study in reading, writing, art, music, social studies and language instruction. Changes in these areas, while not as spectacular as those in science and mathematics, are nonetheless as significant and important. The teaching of history and of geography, however, continue to pose problems since early attempts to combine these in social studies programmes proved less than successful and discouraged many from trying alternative modes of integration of the social sciences. Among the more controversial sectors of the curriculum of the elementary school are the readers to be found there. These continue to provide relatively weak intellectual fare for children, and probably contribute significantly to the distaste for reading among sizeable portions of the school population. The challenges which children meet or do not meet in their beginning school days determine their later academic directions.

TESTS AND EXAMINATIONS

Canadian schoolmen have been prone to favour administering tests and examinations at every level of the educational system. They have been influenced to a considerable degree by the American pattern of achievement and intelligence testing making use of many of the tests originally designed for use in American schools and colleges. More recently there have been attempts made to arrive at Canadian norms for these same tests, but too few Departments of Education or urban school systems have engaged in so doing. Still less has there been the effort to devise tests especially for Canada. Dr. R. W. B. Jackson of the Ontario College of Education did give direction in this respect, and some steps were taken by Dr. Clifford Conway of the Division of Tests and Standards of the British Columbia Department of Education, but again these exercises were inadequate to Canada's needs. All too often there has been the feeling that since these tests were so readily available from just across the border, why go to the trouble and the cost of providing a separate set of tests.

The ten Departments of Education in Canada all administer final examinations for secondary school certification. These examinations are usually prepared by committees made up of principals, teachers, superintendents, and university personnel, and are generally marked by comparable groups. June is generally the period for writing departmental examinations across Canada and August the month during which students generally receive their results. The examinations for terminal academic courses, and for vocational and technical programmes are set by individual schools. Although written examinations predominate throughout the country, there are oral examinations held from time to time, mainly in Quebec, but these are atypical. Most in term and final examinations whether prepared in a department of education, a school or a college, are balanced as to the number of essay and short answer questions. In contrast with European traditions the outside examiner plays a very minor role in either the setting or scoring of school set examinations for terminal programmes. Some school systems, particularly those in urban centres have been moving away from relying exclusively upon the results of final examinations and leaning more towards the practice of continuous assessment of the students' performance throughout the year.

EDUCATIONAL LITERATURE

Until very recently there has been a tremendous dearth of a native Canadian literature on education. Apart from the more or less obvious fact that Canadian educators draw upon the literatures of Europe, Asia and the United States for their sustenance, there has also been the fact that teaching loads, circumstances and climates in Canadian schools, colleges and universities have been such as to preclude the productivity necessary. Despite these limitations, however, there has been a growing body of literature appear, a good sampling of which is noted elsewhere in this volume. The periodical literature has likewise been expanding, and whereas at one time it was limited almost entirely to catering to the needs of the classroom teacher, recent productions have a broader educational spectrum in mind. The *Alberta Journal of Educational Research* and the *Canadian Journal of Education* are but examples of the type of periodical available. In addition, newspapers and popular magazines publishing in Canada have been appointing education reporters with increasing frequency with the result that magazines like *Macleans*, and newspapers like the *Toronto Globe and Mail*, the *Winnipeg Free Press*, the *Montreal Star*, and the *Vancouver Sun* have been devoting considerable attention to education in their columns. Despite the penchant for sensationalism, the newspapers have been providing good coverage of educational developments throughout the country. And while it is still true that topics such as salary negotiations and finance and exploding student populations still capture the headlines, an increasing proportion of space is being devoted to the aims of education, to the curriculum, and to the types of educational institutions deemed most desirable for a particular kind of community.

EDUCATIONAL ORGANIZATIONS

Educational organizations in Canada are many and varied. Home and school and parent–teacher associations are to be found at both national and provincial levels, as is the case with the Canadian Teachers' Federation, the Canadian Association of University Teachers, the School Trustees Association, the Association of Canadian Colleges and Universities, and similar bodies. The Canadian Education Association brings together in one organization ministers and deputy ministers of education, superintendents of urban and rural school systems, supervisors and professors of education. This association is at once one of the oldest and broadest based and most influential educational bodies in Canada. The executive directors of this organization, French and English, have their offices in Toronto and implement the policies spelled out by the Council of Ministers who usually meet once a year in convention. In the main the Canadian Education Association provides the most important platform for the expression of views regarding public education in Canada, and is the body best able to arrange for such co-operation and co-ordination as is possible without jeopardizing the exclusive jurisdictions in education which each minister of education is pledged to guard jealously.

Despite the influence of this Council of Ministers, however, and of the contributions which it has made to Canadian education, this body has been essentially conservative in its policies and in its practices. The ultra-conservatism in 1959 finally prompted a number of leaders in business and industry to take the initiative in convening a series of education conferences designed to bring about radical reforms in the educational scene generally. Although a second Canadian Conference on Education was called in 1962, no more than an exchange of opinion emerged. It became quickly evident that the impetus to achieving some kind of national concensus on educational questions was doomed to defeat before the weight of provincial traditions. However, the 1966 Canadian Education Association Conference witnessed a renewed attempt to provide for a more broadly-based interprovincial educational communication than now obtains. The Canadian Association of Universities and Colleges already provides a central office for the exchange of all information having to do with colleges and universities in Canada, and this example of co-operative endeavour sets an example which responsible authorities cannot entirely ignore.

Educational organizations in Canada came into being in 1840 with the creation of the Society of Schoolmasters in the East, and with the establishment in 1846 of the Reglement de l'Association Des Instituteurs de Montreal. During the late 1800's the Teachers' Association of Canada West (Ontario) came into being, as did the Teachers' Federation of Prince Edward Island in 1880, the Protestant Teachers of Quebec in 1864, the British Columbia Teachers' Federation in 1917, and the Saskatchewan Teachers' Federation in 1933. It is rather interesting to note that the period just prior to Confederation in 1867 and the period following the First World War were periods during which Canadian teachers sought to establish organizations to promote their special interests. In the two decades following the Second World War there has been a significant advance in interorganizational activity to the extent that these organizations see value in pursuing national goals in common.

A NATIONAL OFFICE OF EDUCATION

Canada has been in need of an office of education for a long time, but never more so than now. In 1961 the author stated,

> "It is no longer possible for provincial governments in Canada to carry the sole responsibility for education. Canadian schools, colleges, and especially universities, can no longer be left to the mercies of provincial political expediencies, resources and purposes. Education in Canada at every level is in desperate need of national support, cooperation, and vision. Provincial officials are so busy with provincial matters of education that they have

little time for, let alone concern with, the national need—the realization that Canada is greater than the sum of its provinces."*

Five years later the author still had to write:

"From what has been happening in Canadian education in the past two decades, both at home and abroad, it is clear that provincial and federal agencies are fully aware that the 1867 British North America Act concept of exclusive provincial responsibility for education is no longer tenable. The fact is that education has become not only big business but big politics, and the sooner federal and provincial authorities reconcile their respective responsibilities in this realm the healthier it will be for Canada's educational systems and for Canadians."†

In 1966 the Canadian Education Association's conference began to explore through its Council of Ministers ways and means of establishing machinery which would facilitate the exchange of educational information and at the same time not impinge upon provincial prerogatives. A still more interesting development is the appointment of an officer responsible for educational interests in the Department of State, and even though the terms of reference here are strictly limited, the fact of appointment speaks for itself.

A considerable impetus has been given to the idea of greater federal participation in education by the Economic Council of Canada which in its *Second Annual Review* in 1965 devoted a chapter to education in the course of which education's contribution to Canada's economic growth was analysed and some specific lessons adduced. Said the authors of the report:

"Education is a crucially important factor contributing to economic growth and to rising living standards. This has been the conclusion of a growing body of economic analysis in a number of countries. This is the conclusion also reached in our exploratory analysis of the contribution to the growth of the Canadian economy and to the welfare of its people." (p. 71)

* Joseph Katz, This country needs a national office of education, *Canadian Commentator*, November 1961, p. 12.

† Joseph Katz, Where Canada avoids international cooperation, *Commentator*, January 1966, p. 14.

and further, in a rather interesting analysis of the educational component of the labour force and comparison with that of the United States:

> "The average number of years of schooling among the Canadian male labour force, which had been slightly less than seven years in 1911, had risen to slightly over nine years by 1961—an increase of only about two and a half years over half a century, or less than 7 per cent per decade and about one half of one per cent per year." (p. 77)

and continues:

> "Average years of education per person in the male labour force rose rapidly and fairly steadily from 1910 to 1960 in the United States, with gains of approximately 9 to 10 per cent in each decade over this half century. The Canadian increases were somewhat more uneven and also were consistently below those in the United States. As a consequence, it is estimated that while average years of schooling increased by less than two-fifths in Canada, the comparable increase in the United States was about three-fifths. Thus, a widening education gap has developed between the two countries over these fifty years." (p. 80)*

It is entirely probable that the pace at which social, economic, political, scientific and technological developments have been taking place that a Canadian Office of Education will be a reality in the not too distant future. Whether or not such an office will come in time to compensate for real losses suffered to date is another matter.

INTERNATIONAL ACTIVITIES

Canada's educational role in international affairs had an early beginning in the seventeenth century when French–English relations included accommodation of the school systems of both societies. Canadian participation in the Boer War of 1905, the First World War of 1914–18, and the Second World War of 1939–45 stimulated concern for international action of another and more peaceable form. Although Canadian schools had attracted students from abroad for years, a noteworthy increase

---

* Economic Council of Canada, *Second Annual Review*, Chapter IV, Education and Economic Growth, Ottawa, December 1965, pp. 71ff.

began in the first decade after the Second World War. The 289 students in Canada from countries other than the United States, the United Kingdom, the British West Indies, and Newfoundland increased to approximately 9000. This student number continues to increase, and will in all likelihood continue to do so for some time.

The Canadian Department of External Affairs administers six aid programmes by means of which educational assistance is afforded developing countries. These programmes are the Colombo Plan, the West Indies Programme, the Commonwealth Technical Assistance Programme, the Canadian Commonwealth Scholarship and Fellowship Programme, the special Commonwealth Aid to Africa Programme, and the Canadian Programme of Educational Assistance for the French-speaking States of Africa. In addition, the Canada Council, the Canadian National Commission for Unesco, the Canadian University Service Overseas, and more recently the Company of Young Canadians— Canada's version of the Peace Corps—are all engaged in making some kind of educational contribution abroad. The universities for their part have individual programmes which help to provide much needed educational assistance abroad. In 1961 the University of British Columbia sent a team under the able direction of Professor Leslie Wong to the University of Malaya to help establish a School of Business Administration. Other universities in Canada have followed suit with the result that in some instances Canada's educational efforts abroad are in advance of similar efforts at home, to wit the exceptional needs of Canada's underdeveloped northland.

Canada's contributions to education must also take into account Canada's brain drain to the United States. This drain is of long standing and will in all probability continue to be so as long as opportunities in the United States stay in advance of those in Canada. In 1965, Dr. Edward F. Sheffield, Research Director for

* Joseph Katz, Government policy and international education: Canada, in *Governmental Policy and International Education*, edited by Stewart Fraser, New York John Wiley, 1965, pp. 223ff.

the Association of Universities and Colleges of Canada, claimed that students studying in the United States tend to lose contact with Canada and are ripe to be picked off by universities seeking teachers. Although the drain varies from period to period depending upon the relative buoyancy of the two economies, and the relative demand for trained individuals, Canada has steadily contributed to the United States a goodly percentage of its graduating classes each year for several decades. In some periods this overall migration of talent to the United States has approached six hundred a month in Canada, a figure which Canada can hardly afford, and one which explains why provincial governments are constantly sending teams over to Britain and to Europe to recruit skilled and educated immigrants. In 1962 the author wrote:

> "A survey of Canadians engaged in educational pursuits in the United States reveals that their services and offices cover an exceedingly wide range. Canadians resident as long as twenty and thirty years in the United States, have become presidents and heads of university faculties or departments, are in several instances directors of research, have reached the office of vice-president or president in several national organizations, and have assumed the chairmanships of many committees of local, regional or national bodies. Canadians have even reached positions of signal responsibility in the United States Government service, and in several instances have served or are serving on Presidential Advisory Committees."*

Canada's international educational activities have been increasing steadily, but by no means represent what the people and the economy are capable of affording. In 1964 A. A. Fatouros and R. N. Kelson pointed out that

> "in terms of GNP, Canada's contribution to external aid ranks among the lowest. This fact remains even when the figures for grants only, and not loans, are considered. According to a recent United Nations study, official donations from all developed countries have amounted annually in the years 1956 to 1959 to 0·28 per cent of their combined GNP. The corresponding figure for Canada (for 1960, after the increase in Colombo Plan appropriations) is 0·21 per cent of GNP, a figure still lower than the average."†

---

* Joseph Katz, The Canadian contribution to American education, in *Heritage of American Education*, edited by Richard E. Gross, Boston, Allyn and Bacon, 1962, pp. 315ff.

† A. A. Fatouros and R. N. Kelson, *Canada's Overseas Aid. Toronto*, Canadian Institute of International Affairs, 1964, p. 54.

Canada can well afford to do more than is being done, for developing countries. It is entirely probable that the establishment of a federal office of education would do as much for Canada's external aid efforts in education as it could do for education internally.

CHAPTER 10

Plans and Prospects

PIONEER ECONOMY

In many respects Canada is still a pioneering economy satisfied to reap the harvest of nature's bounty of resources and live from day to day on the results of primary efforts. Although the Canadian economy began to industrialize during the First World War, and urban complexes did not become really significant until after the Second World War, neither phenomenon usually associated with planning succeeded in stimulating marked effort in this direction despite significant examples in Europe and Asia. The Economic Council of Canada through its spokesman Dr. John Deutsch is helping to bring about a change in this attitude. The need for planning was spelled out recently in these words:

> "At the turn of the century, about half of our population was working in agriculture and other primary pursuits where physical stamina and sheer energy were essential requirements. Today, agriculture employs less than one tenth of our population, and commercial farming has itself become a large-scale and highly mechanized business which calls for rising levels of managerial and technical competence."*

More efficient and wide-scale planning is needed in education for still another reason:

> "Canada has in relative terms 40 per cent fewer scientists and engineers than the United States. Moreover, Canada is not well supplied with university graduates generally. Between 1956 and 1963, Canada added one worker to her labour force for every six added in the United States, but our universities granted only one bachelor's degree for every twenty granted in the United States."*

---

* John Deutsch, Economic and social planning and education, Address to Canadian Education Associations, September 22 1966.

124

It is obvious that the Canadian educational machine has not been as productive as it might have been, and the only reason it has been able to continue as it has is because of the following facts:

> "Roughly one out of every four engineers and physical scientists now working in Canada has come here from abroad. So have one third of our architects, one fifth of our physicians and surgeons, and one fifth of our computer programmers. The ratio of post-war immigrants to the total workers in these highly skilled occupations is much higher than for the population at large."*

While industrialization and urbanization have combined to create a demand for skilled people which Canadian educational systems were not prepared to provide, the economy turned to immigration for the people it needed. The explosive demand for skilled people in all parts of the world, however, makes it less than ever likely that Canada can continue to rely on imported skills. The provincial outlook is obviously inadequate in conditions which call for national perspectives and planning. The pioneer approach to solving problems on the basis of neighbourly advice and the farmer's almanac is proving a hindrance rather than a help in an age of technology and of science.

PLANNING IN INDUSTRY

Industrial and commercial organizations in Canada, like their counterparts in other parts of the world, have been engaged in planning for several decades. Many of the large business enterprises maintain their own research organizations and planning boards with the result that their business practices are kept in line with advancing technology and market needs. The creation of new markets, and the need to adapt to changing patterns in old markets, has justified the costs involved in supporting these establishments. More than one industry in Canada spends upwards of 1 per cent of its net income on research and planning.

* John Deutsch, Economic and social planning and education, Address to Canadian Education Associations, September 1966.

Companies of the order of Imperial Oil, the T. Eaton Co., the Aluminum Company of Canada, Cominco, Crown Zellerbach are but a few that have benefited from policies broad enough to allow for constant evaluation.

RESEARCH INSTITUTES AND COUNCILS

The lessons taught by business and industry have not entirely been lost on education. The Alberta Educational Research Council under the original leadership of Patrick Dunlop, and the British Columbia Educational Research Council whose first founding president was Joseph Katz, have each demonstrated the potential of these agencies in bringing about change in education. Unfortunately neither of these organizations has had the whole-hearted support of their respective Departments of Education with the result that they have had to depend upon the voluntary support of teachers and trustees who are themselves beholden to the Department for overall educational policies. The Atlantic Provinces and Ontario each have similar research bodies, but in these instances the provincial governments provide supporting funds. More recently there has been developed the Ontario Institute for Studies in Education, a centre for educational research and graduate study which will be allied not only with the Ontario College of Education and the University of Toronto, but will also help the Department of Education and the Department of Higher Education with research and planning. This, the first of such institutes in Canada, has already prompted similar proposals in different parts of Canada. The Research and Development Centres proposed for the United States and already in operation in several regions provide the model for what is contemplated in Canada providing there is the same kind of government financing as is taking place in that country. Apart from the Atkinson Study designed to discover the pattern of further education goals of high school students in Ontario, there have been very few long-term studies in Canada. Most studies have had to do with educational administration and with finances pointing up the fact that there appears to be much more concern with the control of education than with either its process or its product.

THE CANADA COUNCIL

The Canada Council, created by the Federal Government as a result of the recommendations made by the Honorable Vincent Massey whose report on the Arts, Letters and Humanities in Canada had identified a need for such a council, has in the nine years of its existence contributed greatly to "new vistas which need to be developed" as noted in its report for 1961–2:

> "The Canada Council is composed of twenty-one private citizens drawn from all the provinces of Canada and from many different walks of life. None of them is a member of government or a civil servant. They are completely free, with the advice of an experienced and highly competent investment committee, to invest the money that has been entrusted to them, and to make their own decisions about grants and awards in the programmes of assistance authorized by the Canada Council Act."*

The vistas encompassed by the Council in that year provided for "37·5 per cent of its grants to scholarships and fellowships in the Humanities, 37·5 per cent in the Social Sciences, and 25 per cent in the Arts". In addition to providing these grants the Council also founded projects designed to promote the development of theatres, the establishment of new literary periodicals, research abroad for poets and novelists as well as painters, musicians and sculptors. The Council has also projects and conferences promoted by universities and societies of the order of the Canadian Political Science Association, the Indian School of International Studies, the Social Science Research Council of Canada, the World University Service of Canada, the Royal Society of Canada, and the Canadian Research Centre for Anthropology, to name but a few of the many obtaining support. In its foreword to the 1965–6 Annual Report the Council struck the bellwether of its goal when it wrote:

> "As for the humanities and the social sciences, their situation had grown so desperate, compared with that of the physical and biological sciences,

---

* *The Canada Council Annual Report*, 1961–2, p. 53.

that their only hope appeared to lie in an altogether new deal entirely
distinct from that offered by the Council."*

In the same account the Council reports receiving a special
appropriation from Parliament in the amount of $10 million, the
capital and interest of which are to be spent in 10 years, and not
added to the $50 million endowment the interest of which pro-
vides for the Council's basic financing. In the relatively brief
period of its existence, the Canada Council has demonstrated that
there are vistas on Canada's horizons which can only be realized
through the release of energetic imaginations in its human
resources.

RESEARCH SOCIETIES

Several organizations in Canada are engaged in fundamental
research and in supporting it in both private and public institutions. The National Research Council provides operating grants
for biology, chemical and metallurgical engineering, chemistry,
computers, earth sciences, engineering and physics, experimental
psychology, dental research, space research, and for pure and
applied mathematics. The Social Science Research Council of
Canada, far less financially able, seeks to support studies in
sociology, anthropology, psychology, psychiatry and allied fields.
The Medical Research Council and the National Cancer Institute of Canada, as well as the National Heart Foundation, the
Engineering Society of Canada and similar bodies, all seek to
promote and engage in research which will push back the frontiers of knowledge in addition to opening up new perspectives for
Canada's younger generations who wish to remain at home and
do something other than be hewers of wood and drawers of water.
In all too many instances these councils and foundations have had
to go to the public for the funds required to meet their needs and
have not always been able to obtain enough. More recently the
Federal Government has sought to rectify the situation as it did

* *The Canada Council Annual Report*, 1965–66, p. 1.

on special pleading by the Canada Council, but provincial legislatures have been slow to appreciate the very significant contributions to be obtained by affording the support needed.

FEDERAL GOVERNMENT RESEARCH

In addition to providing funds for research through councils
and societies, the Federal Government supports research and
planning in several of its departments. The Departments of
Agriculture, Industry, Forestry, Fisheries, Mines and Technical
Surveys, National Health and Welfare, Northern Affairs and
National Resources, Transport, Veterans Affairs, and National
Defence all support studies of one kind and another. Several of
these departments support studies of basic significance not only
to applied but to pure science as well. Total expenditures on the
physical, life and nuclear sciences is of the order of $350 million a
year. According to the recent report of the Dominion Bureau of
Statistics:

> "Although the Government continues to perform most of this research
> within its own establishments, its support of outside research is increasing:
> in 1961–62 intramural expenditures accounted for 80 per cent of the total
> but by 1964–65 this percentage will have fallen to about 69. The pro-
> portion by Canadian industry, which was 11 per cent in 1961–62 will have
> increased to 20 per cent by 1964–65, and that performed in Canadian
> universities will have increased from 7 per cent to 10 per cent in the same
> comparison."*

Although governmental, industrial and commercial research
efforts have laid the basis for some significant developments in the
agricultural, commercial, industrial, technological and scientific
life of the community, there has been no such effort put forward
on behalf of elementary and secondary education in Canada.
There is evidence though that this gap will have to be closed
before too long. It remains for provincial intransigence to be
overcome.

* *Canada Year Book*, 1965, p. 397.

TECHNOLOGICAL APPLICATIONS

The development of computers and programmed learning devices, as well as closed-circuit radio and television units, has enabled teachers and supervisors to cope with the increasing numbers of students who have been and are staying longer in the secondary school and going on to a junior college, college of technology, or a university. The greater flexibility which has resulted from the use of modern hardware has helped create a school which can better serve the individual needs of its students. The use of reproducing units such as Xerox and mimeograph devices at relatively low cost has made the distribution of information to large student bodies at once more rapid and reasonable. The recognition that the pocket book is a respectable source of information despite its low cost and low key presentation has made it possible for many students to build up their own libraries and made it possible for school libraries to serve a larger student body a wider variety of titles. The relative ease with which vast amounts of information may be transferred to film and stored and transmitted has radically altered the role of libraries and other information centres. All of these technological applications to information gathering, storage and distribution services in Canada has helped immensely in overcoming the inequalities in educational opportunities determined by vast distances and institutions with relatively limited resources.

Dr. G. Neil Perry has suggested that school administrators go modern and begin to use some of the new decision-making tools found so valuable by industry. Said he on one occasion,

> "It would be a great help to educators to have a mathematical model of the education system which we could use to list various suggestions in a simulated way; to test the probable consequences in terms of classrooms, teachers, and other logistical needs, of such a radical change in education policy as the lowering of school entry age to three."*

There is no doubt that educators have a long way to go to

* Dr. G. Neil Perry, Address to Canadian Association of School Superintendents, Vancouver, September 21, 1966.

benefit from the examples set by business and industry in the use of technological and sophisticated devices of various kinds.

STUDENT LOAN PROGRAMME

The Canada Student Loan programme inaugurated in 1964 permits students to borrow up to $1000 a year to a maximum of $5000 for an entire period at a university. Whereas the original amount allotted by the Federal Government for this programme was $40 million, the sum has since been increased to $60 million, with the prospect of an equivalent increase being forthcoming in the next two-year period. Although these are federal funds the scheme is administered by the provincial governments. During the 1965–6 school year Ontario received approximately $19·5 million; Newfoundland, $1·84 million; Prince Edward Island, $369,000; Nova Scotia, $2·5 million; New Brunswick, $2·2 million; Manitoba, $2·9 million; Saskatchewan, $2·9 million; Alberta, $4·2 million; British Columbia, $5·3 million; the Yukon $25,000; and the Northwest Territories, $55,000. These student loans are repayable following graduation and after a student has begun employment. Though the scheme has enabled many students to receive an education, there are several aspects of the plan which need revision. Thus far, however, the scheme has proven to be sufficiently successful to warrant its continuance, and an increase in the amounts of money available to students.

POPULATION INCREASE

According to a survey conducted by the Association of Universities and Colleges of Canada, university enrolment will increase 170 per cent to 553,000 (at present 206,000) students by 1976. It is expected also that the percentage of persons in the 18–24 year age group attending university will increase from 10·1 per cent to 18·6 per cent in the same period. It is estimated that about one-sixth of this group will be engaged in graduate studies. All of these figures suggest that the Canadian educational establishment has to be markedly increased to accommodate both the increase in numbers and the change in emphasis.

The aforementioned figures do not take into account the very real increase which will take place in vocational, technical and adult education programmes which have been showing pronounced increases in attendance. In the adult education sector alone the increase in enrolment between the year 1961–2 and 1962–3 was from 3,281,178 to 3,972,002, an order of increase which may be expected to be surpassed in succeeding years because of retraining requirements due to automation and changing technology.

The pressure of numbers promises to bring about changes in the kinds of physical plants developed, the kinds of programmes offered, and the arrangements of the academic year. Expected also are changes in style of teaching, methods of grouping students in seminar and theatre, and in the time allowed students for self-study.

RELIGION AND THE SCHOOLS

Although denominational schools do provide for those children whose parents wish more religious teachings than the public school affords, there are those who urge more attention to religion in the public schools themselves. One school of thought holds that public schools ought not to concern themselves with any kind of religious teaching beyond a mere reading of passages of the Bible without comment of any kind. Another school of thought holds that even this is uncalled for. A third school holds that class hours should be allowed for the study of Judaism, Buddhism, Mohamedism, Confucianism as well as Christianity. In general, few are satisfied with present arrangements, though no one has come up with an idea as to how to provide for a study of values without at the same time impinging upon the grounds of dogma.

The public schools in all provinces have been extremely careful to avoid any kind of charge that they were presenting the dogma of any particular religion in contravention of the non-religious character of the schools. Nonetheless, general concern with the need to have children and youth given sets of values beyond those normally dealt with in literature, history and counselling programmes makes for the reopening of this contentious question from time to time. The prospect is that the question will continue to receive attention.

PENITENTIARY PROGRAMMES

The Stony Mountain Penitentiary in Manitoba has pioneered a Canadian educational programme for prisoners designed to rehabilitate inmates through education. The basic training programme is designed to equip students with academic skills in English, mathematics and science as a prerequisite for advanced vocational training. According to George Tegman, assistant deputy warden in charge of inmate training, one major purpose is to provide a training programme that will assist prisoners in preparing for a successful reintroduction into community life. Approximately 50 per cent of the prison population of 450 attend classes five mornings a week, taking one of three kinds of programme leading to certificates for the completion of Grade 7, 10 and 11.

The response to this programme, originally developed in the United States where it has enjoyed successful attendance, has been so encouraging as to suggest to prison wardens of other institutions the desirability of having similar courses. In all probability educational programmes for prisons can benefit from the use of the newer technologies in the form of closed-circuit television programmes, programmed learning, and similar techniques.

SEX EDUCATION

For the past several years medical people, social workers, guidance personnel and parent–teacher associations have been calling for some form of sex education in the schools. Although biology, botany, chemistry, health and physical education courses do provide for some aspects of sex education, there is little that can be called comprehensive in any way. The family life and sex education programmes developed in Sweden serve as the model for the recommendations being made but thus far Departments of Education have been hesitant about moving into this area. Despite this hesitancy, however, it is likely that some form of these programmes will have to be introduced if the needs of the young people are to be served.

Since 1953 there has been an increase of 175 per cent in the number of boys and girls of juvenile age brought before the courts. Juveniles are in general under 16 years of age. The age group 7–12 years accounted for 22·9 per cent of those considered delinquent; the age group 13–15 accounted for 76·2 per cent of the group. Again, although the age group 16–24 years constitutes only 18·7 per cent of the total population, they account for over 50 per cent of indictable offences, among which are those of sex of one kind and another.

The aforementioned figures suggest that the concern with sex education is a concern with the broad perspective of values in many realms of the lives of youth, and programmes developed in the one area will be designed to cover other areas as well.

THE EXPLODING FUTURE

Over the years Canada's educational enterprise expanded at a rate sufficient to enable it to provide a relatively adequate elementary and secondary schooling for its population but had to rely upon the products of European and British schools to staff its institutions. Not until after the First World War did the Canadian educational systems provide anything like the number of vocationally and technically trained people required by the developing society, and even then had to import some of the skilled people necessary to industrial and commercial expansion.

The demands made upon the Canadian economy engendered by the Second World War spurred many educational developments including the recognition that a modern technological society can only be created by people trained in technological institutes and educated in universities and colleges prepared to involve students in ongoing research. It was in this period, too, that both provincial and federal governments, and even some industrial and commercial organizations, began to recognize that investment in education was just as important, if not more important, as investment in roads, bridges and garbage disposal units; that human resources were just as valuable as natural resources and needed cultivation on as grand a scale.

At the same time, all agencies recognized that developments in the social sciences suggested revisions in elementary and secondary education patterns to enable the sophisticated young urbanite to sense as much challenge in the school as he could find in the community; and to make it possible for the rural student to benefit from academic and vocational programmes on a basis of equality with his urban cousin. Developments in the fields of sociology, anthropology, psychology and psychiatry were incorporated, albeit slowly, in the methodology of the schools. Despite these adaptations, however, Canadian schools still depend for the bulk of their innovations upon the research studies of other countries, particularly those conducted in the United States and Great Britain.

Federal, provincial and municipal governments are all sensitive to the new power being exercised by educational agencies, and the professional bodies in and out of government in Canada are attempting to respond to the educational needs of the country on a pragmatic basis. Unfortunately the pragmatic approach, if limited in its perspective, excludes the advantages to be gained from careful planning with the result that progress is very uneven across the country. Although it is recognized that the new technology in communication can make for greater unity of endeavour, local prejudice and provincialism precludes the kind of co-operation essential to a more or less uniform advance in Canadian education. The introduction of educational TV, job retraining programmes on a federal basis, the development of a wide variety of community college opportunities, these and similar developments have failed to compensate for the ill effects of making education the playboy of politics.

Despite some of the restrictions which have impeded educational developments there are in progress a sufficient number of projects in the field of education to recognize that the society as a whole is pushing forward as far as possible under the circumstances. The universities in particular have been engaged in forward-looking planning in keeping with their penchant for pushing back the frontiers of knowledge. A recent cross-Canada survey revealed that well over $600 million worth of projects were in progress including the development of new libraries, planetaria, atom smashers, astronomical observatories, computer centres, health and physical education areas, medical science complexes, mathematics and science centres. The universities are also placing much more emphasis upon graduate work than heretofore in recognition of the fact that not only have human resources to be cultivated to their highest potential, but that it is no longer possible for Canada to remain a parasite in the field of professional and advanced studies.

The urban centres in Canada have been at the forefront of educational advance in Canada in elementary, secondary, vocational, technical, technological and adult education programmes. City school administrations such as are to be found in Toronto, Edmonton and Vancouver have broken new ground in devising new curricula, new school programmes, and generally adopting an experimental approach considerably in advance of provincial Departments of Education which continue to remain unnaturally conservative and limited by political considerations. Because Departments of Education also continue to dominate teacher education programmes despite the move of these programmes to university campuses, teacher education lags in many respects and represents an unrealized potential in Canada. Many urban school systems have adopted the practice of in-service programmes to keep their teachers abreast of developments in the system and in the field. In Canada, as elsewhere, the future belongs to the city, and it is in these centres of population that educational advances will continue to take place. One of Canada's real obstacles to further progress is the imbalance between the rurally-dominated legislatures which still control education, and the needs of the rapidly developing urban societies who are politically—and educationally—disenfranchised.

Bibliography

ADAMS, HOWARD. *The Education of Canadians*. Montreal: Harvest House, 1968.
ALTHOUSE, J. G. *Structure and Aims of Canadian Education*. Toronto: W. J. Gage, 1949.
ANDREWS, J. H. M. and BROWN A. F., (eds.) *Composite High Schools in Canada*. Edmonton: University of Alberta, 1959.
AUDET, A. L. *Le Système Scolaire de la Province de Quebec*. Quebec: Erable and Laval, 1956.
BARNARD, H. C. *The French Tradition in Education*. Cambridge University Press, 1922.
BELL, W. N. *The Development of the Ontario High School*. Toronto: University of Toronto Press, 1918.
CAMPBELL, H. L. *Curriculum Trends in Canadian Education*. Toronto: W. J. Gage, 1952.
CANADA: Report on Developments in Education: 1965–66. *Canadian Education and Research Digest*, Vol. 6, No. 2, June 1966, pp. 79–93.
Canada Year Book, 1965, 1966.
CANADIAN COUNCIL OF CHURCHES. *Religious Education in Schools of Canada*. Toronto: Canadian Council, 1963.
CHEAL, JOHN E. *Investment in Canadian Youth*. Toronto: Macmillan, 1963.
COUTTS, H. T. A Mari Usque Ad Mare: Educational Problems. *Canadian Education and Research Digest*, Vol. 6, No. 4, December 1966.
DOMINION BUREAU OF STATISTICS. *A Graphic Presentation of Canadian Education*. Ottawa: Queen's Printer, 1961.
DOMINION BUREAU OF STATISTICS. *Survey of Vocational Education and Training*, 1959–60. Ottawa, 1961.
DOMINION BUREAU OF STATISTICS. *The Organization and Administration of Public Schools in Canada*. Ottawa, 1966.
FRECKER, G. A. *Education in the Atlantic Provinces*. Toronto: W. J. Gage, 1956.
GAITSKELL, C. D. and GAITSKELL, MARGARET R. *Art Education in the Kindergarten*. Toronto: Ryerson Press, 1952.
GILLETT, MARGARET. *A History of Education*. Toronto: McGraw-Hill, 1966.
GOVERNMENT OF CANADA. Department of Labour. Economics and Research Branch. *Working and Living Conditions in Canada*. Ottawa: Queen's Printer, 1964.
GOVERNMENT OF CANADA. Department of Labour. National Employment Service. *Supply and Demand: University Graduates, 1965–66*. Ottawa: Queen's Printer, 1966.
HARRIS, RONALD S. *A Bibliography of Higher Education in Canada*. Toronto: University of Toronto Press, 1960.

HUMBLE, A. H. *The Crisis in Canadian Education.* Toronto: Ryerson, 1959.

JACKSON, R. W. B. *Educational Research in Canada.* Toronto: Gage & Co., 1961.

JOHNSON, F. H. *A Brief History of Canadian Education.* Toronto: McGraw-Hill, 1968.

KATZ, JOSEPH. *Canadian Education Today.* Toronto: McGraw-Hill, 1956.

KATZ, JOSEPH. *Elementary Education in Canada.* Toronto: McGraw-Hill, 1961.

KIDD, JAMES R. *Adult Education in Canada.* Canadian Association for Adult Education: Toronto, 1950.

LANG, S. *Education and Leisure.* Toronto: J. M. Dent, 1930.

LAYCOCK, S. R. *Mental Hygiene in the School.* Vancouver: Copp-Clark, 1960.

LAYCOCK, S. R. *Special Education in Canada.* Toronto: Gage & Co., 1963.

LAZERTE, M. E. *School Finance in Canada.* Edmonton: Hamly Press, 1955.

LAZERTE, M. E. *Teacher Education in Canada.* Toronto: W. J. Gage, 1951.

LINDEMAN, EDWARD C. *The Meaning of Adult Education.* Montreal: Harvest House, 1961.

LLOYD, WOODROW S. *The Role of Government in Canadian Education.* Toronto: W. J. Gage, 1959.

MACKINNON, FRANK. *The Politics of Education.* Toronto: University of Toronto Press, 1960.

MOFFATT, H. P. *Educational Finance in Canada.* Toronto: Gage, 1957.

MORTON, W. L. *The Canadian Identity.* Toronto: The University of Toronto Press, 1961.

NEATBY, HILDA. *So Little for the Mind.* Toronto: Clarke, Irwin, 1953.

NEATBY, HILDA. *The Debt of Our Reason.* Toronto: Clarke, Irwin, 1954.

PARK, JULIAN. *The Culture of Contemporary Canada.* Toronto: Ryerson Press, 1957.

PATON, JAMES M. *The Role of Teachers' Organizations in Canadian Education.* Toronto: W. J. Gage, 1962.

PERCIVAL, W. S. *Should We All Think Alike?* Toronto: Gage & Co., 1952.

PHILLIPS, C. E. *Public Secondary Education in Canada.* Toronto: W. J. Gage, 1955.

PHILLIPS, C. E. *The Development of Education in Canada.* Toronto: W. J. Gage, 1957.

PORTER, JOHN. *The Vertical Mosaic.* Toronto: The University of Toronto Press, 1965.

RATTE, ALICE and GAGNON, GILLBERTE. *Bibliographic Analytique de la Litterature Pedagogique Canadianne-Francaise.* Montreal: Centre de Psychologie, 1952.

REEVES, ARTHUR W. (Ed.) *The Canadian School Principal.* Toronto: McClelland and Stewart, 1962.

RENNEY, ARTHUR J. *Some Aspects of Rural Education in Canada.* Toronto: University of Toronto Press, 1950.

ROWE, F. N. *The History of Education in Newfoundland.* Toronto: Ryerson Press, 1952.

RUSSELL, D. H. *Implications of Research for Canadian Class Room.* Toronto: W. J. Gage, 1953.

SCHRAMM, W. L. *Television in the Lives of Our Children.* Toronto: University of Toronto Press, 1961.

SEELEY, J. R., R. A. LOOSELY and E. W. SIM. *Crestwood Heights.* Toronto: University of Toronto Press, 1956.

SHACK, SYBIL. *Armed With a Primer.* Toronto: McClelland and Stewart, 1965.

SISSONS, C. B. *Church and State in Canadian Education.* Toronto: Ryerson, 1959.

SKINNER, ANDREW F. Philosophy of Education in Canada. *Canadian Education and Research Digest*, December 1963.

STEWART, F. K. and FLOWER, G. E. *Leadership in Action: The Superintendent of Schools in Action.* Toronto: W. J. Gage, 1958.

SWIFT, W. H. *Trends in Canadian Education.* Toronto: Gage, 1958.

TREMBLAY, JACQUES. *Lieux Communs sur l'Education.* Quebec: Presses Universitaire Laval, 1958.

Vocational and Technical Training for Girls at High School, post High School and Trade School Levels of Education in Canada. Women's Bureau. Department of Labour: Ottawa, 1963. Pp. vi 95.

Index

148 *Index*